There Used To Be a *Fish* Called Salmon

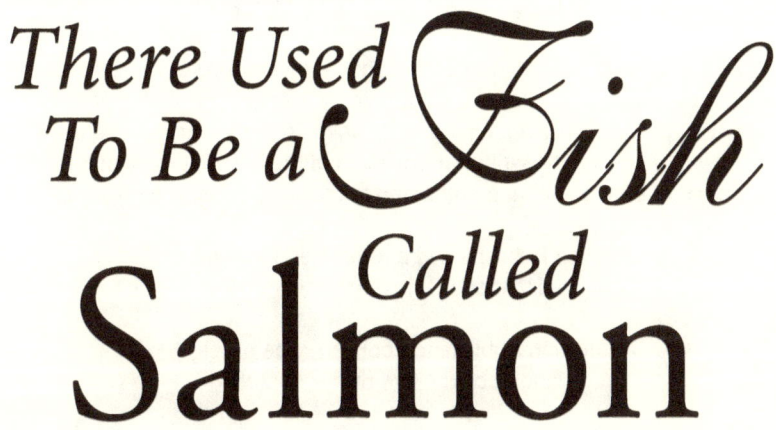

*A Collection of Short Stories,
Poems, and Story-Poems*

Teresa M. Mosteller

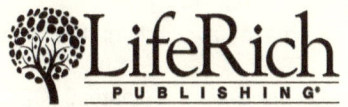

LifeRich
PUBLISHING

LifeRich Publishing is a registered trademark of
The Reader's Digest Association, Inc.

LifeRich Publishing books may be ordered
through booksellers or by contacting:

LifeRich Publishing
1663 Liberty Drive
Bloomington, IN 47403
www.liferichpublishing.com
1 (888) 238-8637

ISBN: 978-1-4897-0737-6 (sc)
ISBN: 978-1-4897-0771-0 (hc)
ISBN: 978-1-4897-0738-3 (e)

Library of Congress Control Number: 2016903788

Print information available on the last page.

LifeRich Publishing rev. date: 05/12/2016

~ INTRODUCTION ~

When I decided to submit this manuscript for publication, I wasn't sure how to describe it. Is it a simple poetry book, an anthology, a collection, or something else entirely? What it is, is a Valentine that encompasses my caring family, my dear friends, my hopes; dreams; disappointments; and this wacky, wonderful life that I'm grateful to have and that I've chosen to celebrate within these humble pages. It is submitted with admiration, slight apprehension, and a small dose of frustration toward what has always been my primary source of inspiration -- the written word.

Words fascinate me. Writing has been a favorite pastime almost since the time I started to read. As a child I found the practice of writing poems therapeutic, and would write when I was feeling lonely or sad. The results of my efforts always managed to lift my spirits, even if I chose not to share what I'd written with others.

It didn't take long to discover that I enjoyed the art of writing. Eventually, I wanted to become better at it. I would strive to find the right word, delighting in each small success. I'd spend hours crafting a rhyming poem, doing my best to fine-tune it while also preserving its integrity and meaning. (These are a writer's lifetime works in progress.)

Soon I began to write poems and verses for family members' birthdays. Then I wrote poetry for friends. I didn't limit myself to poetry, either -- I've written short stories and essays, and I've mounted several original one-act plays. I submitted an original comedy script and directed it for the Seattle Playwrights' Festival. Recently several family members and I collaborated on an original play and performed it at the Tabor Opera House in Leadville, Colorado. That was a particular high point for us.

Throughout the years I've written whenever the spirit has moved me. It has moved me a lot.

Curiously, my very first love of the written word – my love for writing poems – could more aptly be called a love/hate relationship. In my preteens I wrote a small book of poetry (one poem for each month of the year) and showed it to my dad, who loved it. Then I showed it to my mom, who also gave it a "thumbs-up." That was high praise. As my confidence grew, I shared the poems with the rest of my family and some of my friends, whose positive reactions were encouraging.

Later I brought my book to school, and was delighted to see that others could relate to what I had written. However, one girl in my class slammed my work. She was particularly critical of the poem that happened to be my personal favorite. Her words hurt, and I was almost apologetic for having shared it. Although my family continued to offer encouragement, self-doubt reared its ugly head. I started to feel like a fraud. Would I ever again be able to capture the "brilliance" of my early efforts? And, if I was so negatively affected by even one person who found fault with my work, what was the point in trying? What if others hated it, too? At any rate, the die was cast. Although I kept writing (for therapy), that first book of poems no longer gave me joy. Eventually, it got buried along with other assorted rubble at the bottom of a box.

Years later, I was clearing clutter during a move and stumbled across it. Rereading my old favorite poem still brought a twinge of pain – but this time, the hurt was caused by the recognition of my own cowardice! I suddenly felt ashamed. I had spent years burying my passion, inwardly finding excuses that no longer made sense.

This mini-anthology of poems and short stories is my effort to remedy that. I'm certainly old enough to have learned a thing or two, and blessedly young enough to keep trying. It's fun to share the things we (think we) know, and in so doing to discover kindred spirits who will connect with our experiences and find some common ground. When we share our stories with others, we allow others to know us a little better. I'd like to think we also become better for it.

With love,
Teresa

PS: Scattered throughout this book are several poems I wrote years ago on the topic of unrequited love. These early efforts now feel like tales from a former life (or someone else's life). For example, "Willie, I Understand" is a tongue-in-cheek lament about repeatedly falling for the wrong guy; and "Mister Twister" is a brief analogous exercise that compares a relationship-gone-wrong to a thrilling but nauseating amusement-park ride. These poems helped lead me to a place of self-discovery and wholeness, which is why I chose to include them. This book would not be complete otherwise.

~ ACKNOWLEDGMENTS ~

I gratefully dedicate this book to
my husband Gordy,
my daughter Emily,
my son Thomas,
and our cats Casey and Bastet.
You are my life, my love, my joy, my wisdom,
and my constant inspiration. God bless you.

A world of loving thanks to
my siblings Mayo, Margaret,
Daniel, Angel and Johnny
and my brothers-in-law Ed and Mel

Love to my future son-in-law Colin,
along with his kind & generous family;
and to family members
John, Jimmy, Anne-Marie, Mary, George,
Dick, James, Day and Tesa
Karen M.
Linda & Randy; Ben & Hil
David & Margo; Tony;
Christopher & Tiffaney; Jack and Ty
Mary H., Mary & Brent W.; Riley; Patrick and Killian
Tracy, Brian and Mike

Deep appreciation for
the many friends who have encouraged
me to keep working on my craft, especially
Tricia, Nancy B., Nancy D.,
Paula, Maydene, Andy, Bill, Rose,
Lisa, Mary, Sue, Barb, Annie & Dawn

Honorable mentions to
My Educational Tour Buddies
My co-workers past & present
My theatre cohorts and Playhouse NW
My choir peeps
The folks on my Facebook page
The many writers who have entertained,
inspired and taught me

Love & R.I.P.
My parents Teresa & Robert
My sister Mara
Kathleen O.
(Great-Great) Grandma Mary
(Grand)pa Jerry
Aunt Phyl & Uncle Bud
Beloved pets Thespis, Kahlua, Chelsea;
and all of the loving pets who
nurtured us during childhood

There Used to Be a Fish Called Salmon

~ TABLE OF CONTENTS ~

<u>January</u>

~ *An Afternoon at the Movies* ~

She wiped the rain-washed moisture
From her burgundy cloth jacket
And sprinted toward the steel-rimmed booth.
There was a touch of chill
In the chalky-gray atmosphere
With just a tease of late-afternoon sun
Attempting to break through the milky-thick stratus layer.

As she hastened toward the concession counter
She felt the tingle of keys and loose coins in her pocket
And secured her blue-and-white ticket there.
Reese's® Pieces, Raisinettes®, M&Ms®
and Snickers® awaited her.
Graduated stacks of cylindrical purple-
and-yellow popcorn bins
Lined the booth against the wall
And a mound of freshly-popped kernels
Sat inside a clear plastic-covered, metal-based popper.
The avalanche of snow-covered golden nuggets,
Having blissfully burst forth only moments before,
Was now silent, while the cruelly tempting
Aromatic fragrance of warm buttered corn lingered.

Following the scrunch-scrunch of the
snowy nuggets into the bin
And the fzzzzt-fzzzzt-fzzzzt-tap-
tap-tap of the soda fountain,
She traded change and lurched
hurriedly toward the winding,
Newly deserted hallway with her
delectable sweets in one hand
While, with her free hand, she anxiously rummaged
For the security of the soft cardboard
ticket in her pocket.
Whew. It was there, nestled snugly
against her jangling keys.
Forgetting what she came to see
She gave the ticket a reassuring look,
and felt momentarily relieved
As she dodged into the nearest auditorium
Just as the lights dimmed.

After adjusting her eyes to the darkened surroundings
She settled into a cushiony crimson velvet seat
And reached for a single kernel of popcorn...
Ahhh! It melted invitingly in her mouth.
She sat back and relaxed.
As the familiar Fox searchlights lit up the huge screen,
She knew she was home.
The afternoon's drama was at an end.
The motion picture was about to begin.

~ THE BEACON ~

Mary was a gifted artist, an avid gardener, a fine storyteller, and a purveyor of Puget Sound history. She was the matriarch of five generations. Mary kept a tidy home, and for a long time she had a cat named Maui. The cat was sleek and lovely, but also ornery. She would bite and scratch indiscriminately and without notice, sometimes while purring. But she loved Mary, and Mary loved her. Mary (who became "Grandma" to me) always gave us fair warning about Maui's violent tendencies, but the two of them shared a mutual respect and understanding.

Grandma's belongings were few and precious. When she passed away at the age of 102, we noticed she had kept a gift that had been given to her by my daughter -- her great-granddaughter Emily. On Grandma's 100th birthday, my daughter, a pastry artist, baked her a cake and crafted a lighthouse topping. Grandma ate the cake (with help from her family and friends) but she held onto the lighthouse. Grandma didn't want us to make a lot of fuss on her 100th birthday, but she was gracious and appreciative on that special day.

Lighthouses are navigational aids that, with their luminescent beacons, serve to warn ships away from danger and help to guide the vessels safely to harbor. Lighthouses are individually unique structures -- statuesque, artistic and fascinating. Although their usefulness may be considered somewhat "old-fashioned" by today's high-tech navigational standards, they are appreciated all over the world for their historic landmark status, their merits with seagoing travelers, and their singular artistic craftsmanship.

Grandma loved lighthouses, and we all knew it. We inundated her with lighthouse knick-knacks and memorabilia. She collected them for years until she sold her house and moved to an island retirement home in her later years. While contented there, she no longer had room for all the lighthouse photos, framed prints, cards, books, statues, salt-&-pepper shakers, Christmas ornaments, needlepoint pillows, aprons, calendars, and other do-dads and assorted items that she had collected or that had been given to her as gifts over her considerable lifetime. Yet this uncluttered soul held onto a few choice pieces (including the cake decoration) until her dying day.

Grandma Mary was a quiet and petite, yet sturdy strength of a woman. She wisely and lovingly presided over several generations of career mariners. Like the lighthouses she admired so much, Grandma was an illuminating protector and beacon of hope; like them, she was artistic, lovely, and uniquely timeless.

~ *Hope* ~

There I was, feeling miserable

Thinking of only myself again, as usual

When I got this irresistible urge to call a friend

And something I happened to say managed to make his whole day

This is the moment that makes life worthwhile

Suddenly, there's a reason for tomorrow.

~ Model Car ~

50's Corvette
Convertible
Pristine shape
Fine detail
Leather seats
Chrome fenders
Aerodynamic dashboard
Door with solid click
Gorgeous cherry-red body
Custom black trim
Roomy trunk space
Whitewall tires
Doesn't run on gas
It runs on passion

Silently, stealthily ~ the only sounds
Are the wind and the speakers
S-w-e-e-t ride
Gliding smoothly and effortlessly
Around a curve
Easily wiping out the competition
The track is clear
The race is over
My 'vette is the hands-down winner
Swarmed by impressed onlookers
Then placed in the palm
Of my lucky hand
She settles again in a prominent place
On my bookshelf

~ *Our Loving Mom* ~

Nothing in our vast array
Of introspections can convey
The boundless, brilliant workings of her mind.
Her dad worked for the railroad.
She honored a strict moral code
With disciplined and willful streaks entwined.
She taught us to "ar-TIC-u-late."
She once joined the novitiate.
Her good deeds bordered on a sacrifice.
Mom held an open world view.
She made a wicked Irish stew.
She'd balk when total strangers called her *nice.*
Mom loved it when we'd see a show
Could make a wilting flower grow
(The greenness of her thumb was fairly grand).
She sent us all to private school.
Both taught and lived the Golden Rule.
A southpaw, she could write with either hand.
"Won't climb a mountain – 'cuz it's there."
And yet, she took us everywhere.
We'd grab "a little something" good to eat.
Mom's agonies and ecstasies
imparted vivid memories
That were eccentric, real and concrete.
Impulsive but forgiving, she
would scold us euphemistically.
Fiercely protective, deigning to forbid.
When we were relatively small
We joked that she'd outlive us all
Amazingly, I kind of think she did.

~ *Seven Brides for Seven Brothers for Seven Years* ~

A grand and glorious movie,
And now a Denver show!
My sister bought us tickets
I gladly said I'd go.

The playhouse had a scandal
Production was shut down
(I flew to Denver anyway,
Since I am from that town).

And then, just one year later,
The Fifth* announced its season.
I bought two ticket packages
With ...*Brides...* as the main reason.

The gift was for my daughter.
I rented a hotel.
Our dinner, show and downtown stay
Were planned so very well.

The day of the performance,
A snowstorm welcomed us
So, warned to skip the icy roads,
We chose to take a bus.

We stood there for three hours
Until our toes were numb.
A futile try – all wasted on
A bus that didn't come.

To this day, after all this time
(As soon as it appears)
With baited breath, we'll see this show!
We've waited seven years.

*Fifth Avenue Theater, Seattle, WA

February

~ 1982 ~

Having finished all of my college credits a few weeks earlier, but with graduation four months away, I was ready for the adventure of a lifetime. A few months previously on a whim, I had applied for a passport, purchased an airline ticket to England, and traveled to London by myself. It was the impetus I needed to have some vague idea regarding what I wanted to do with the rest of my life. Less than six months later on a cold February day, I bought a one-way ticket to Seattle, Washington, the home of one of my sisters. It was the first and only time I traveled somewhere without planning to return. I left with the blessing of my Colorado family, so I knew my choice was the right one.

My sister and her husband greeted me at the airport, welcomed me warmly, and invited me to live in their West Seattle home for those first critical months in my new hometown. During my first evening in Seattle, they treated me to dinner and dessert at a very nice restaurant on the city's popular waterfront. A few short weeks later, they shared some exciting news: they were expecting a baby! It would be their first.

As June approached, I worried and wondered whether I should fly back home to attend my college commencement ceremony. I decided to pass. I had a job by then, and didn't want to risk my reputation with my employer by requesting time off so soon after starting. My diploma arrived in the mail about a month after the ceremony. To ease my disappointment in having missed that momentous occasion, my sister and her husband once again took me out to dinner to celebrate! They made me feel very special over the arrival of that piece of paper.

The remainder of the year was eventful. In November, my Boulder boyfriend surprised me with an impromptu visit to Seattle. My mom had flown to Seattle to help my sister prepare for the birth of her beautiful baby boy. The house was suddenly a cluttered flurry of activity with my sister, her husband, their baby, my mom, my boyfriend, and me sharing a space that only a few months earlier had been occupied by two.

One morning a few days after my mom's arrival, she walked into my sister's kitchen to fix breakfast and help with the dishes. My boyfriend had several bottles of vitamins spread out on the counter, which piqued my mom's curiosity. When she began to question his extensive use of vitamins and pills, an interesting exchange ensued between them.

Boyfriend: My parents ruined my life.

Mom: How did they do that?

BF: They fed me white sugar and white flour.

Mom: Sugar and flour? What exactly did they feed you?

BF: *(visibly irritated and indignant):* I **told** you! White sugar and white flour!

Mom: *(equally irritated and indignant):* ***In what form?*** They didn't just place a bowl of white sugar and white flour in front of you!

BF: They fed me boxed cereal, white bread, crackers, cookies, pies...food like that.

Mom *(pulling herself up and sighing in mock horror):* ***Well!*** Those dirty, rotten, no-good sons of bitches!

My boyfriend sat stunned and speechless, and his self-righteous attitude instantly dissolved. To this day, whenever we witness someone overly critical of someone else for an unintended slight, we secretly conjure up Mom's well-timed retort.

Following that fun bit of drama, the six of us managed to harmoniously celebrate Christmas together in Seattle. It was the first of many happy holidays that I've spent in the Pacific Northwest. The occasion was blessedly joyful, made even more so with a newborn baby to remind us of the vital reason for the season. We delighted in watching the ferries and cruise vessels sailing across Elliott Bay, decked out with Christmas lights and decorations. Sometimes we heard the sweet sounds of Christmas music playing from the boats.

Not long afterward, I would find a place of my own in Bellevue (a growing metropolis east of Seattle) and my independence in God's country would truly begin. Less than a year later, I would find myself back in West Seattle, living on my own. I settled in West Seattle for good. I was home.

The year 1982 will always remain precious to me. I miss my home town of Colorado and the people who live there, and try to see them often. We all do. But I will always be happy for that out-of-the-blue whim that led to a risk, which became a fulfilling adventure of a lifetime.

~ *The Color of love* ~

True love is not blue
For sadness comes not from loving,
But from not being loved in return.

True love is not red like a heart
For a heart can be broken,
But true love can never be broken.

Love is not green like the trees and the forests
For these can lose their lives,
But true love can never die.

Love is not clear like a tear
For I have cried too many tears,
Yet I have not, and cannot, love too much.

No, love is not a color, for if it were
I'd have chosen every color of the rainbow
And given each one to you.

But for you I felt sadness, and heartbreak, and tears,
And a little of my life went with you
When you went away...

And you never knew that I loved you.

~ *GO, BRONCOS!* ~

As a little person, I wasn't much into spectator sports. My favorite sports were basketball and volleyball (not to watch; to play). Living in the Mile-High city, I'd heard of this football team called the Broncos, but didn't know enough about football to care; plus, people would make jokes about the Broncos' ineffectiveness on the field. (There's the one about the guy who is super smart and wants to be more like his friends, so he inserts a dumbing-down serum into his arm – and then he falls asleep without removing it. When his friends find him several days later, he's sitting there babbling, "Go, Broncos. Go, Broncos. Go, Broncos....")

In my youth the Broncos rarely made it into the playoffs -- and forget about the Super Bowl. I was therefore surprised to learn that Broncos tickets had been sold out for years. Season tickets were untouchable; the waiting list was something like 20 years. Well, being younger than 20 at the time, I could barely comprehend that kind of loyalty. I asked my brother-in-law why the team was so popular since they always lost. After he removed the smoke from his ears, he said Denver had the most loyal, die-hard fans in the world. And don't ever think otherwise. He said the Broncos would get on the board someday and make history with a win. Just you wait and see, he said. Have faith.

They did do that, for the first time, in 1998. Super Bowl XXXII. They repeated the feat one year later, at Super Bowl XXXIII.

My mom was a huge Broncos fan, and she was on her deathbed during that first win. She slept through most of the game, but when she learned they'd won, her last words on earth were "*Thank* God!!" (Sarcastic, but thoroughly sincere -- that was Mom to the end.) I truly believe she died happy.

The Broncos made history again in 2016. Although I was disappointed that my Seahawks didn't get to the Super Bowl for the third straight year, I was ecstatic for Denver's team. The Broncos went on to WIN the landmark 50th Super Bowl (as underdogs, no less!). It was a testament to their fans' amazing team spirit, and some awesome ball-playing by Peyton Manning & company.

~ A Heartless Valentine ~

I'd see him walking down the hall
He was quite thin and very tall
I never thought about him twice
To him, I was as cold as ice
But then one day on my lunch break
I sat with him for my friend's sake
She introduced us then and there
And I could not avoid his stare
Soon he was chasing long and hard
On Valentine's I got his card
And then we started going out
And after that? I had no doubt!
He made me laugh and we had fun
He soon became my number one
But then one day we grew apart
I could not hold onto his heart
For his heart yearned for someone new
And there was nothing I could do
I lie at night and call his name
But he is with another dame
And all that's left of him that's mine
Is one small, heartless Valentine
And when I look at it, I sting
For now, it doesn't mean a thing.

~ I Especially Love ~

The single, bright sunflower in a floral bouquet
An inside joke that connects old friends
The fuzziness of a newborn's cheek
Welcome wag of a dog's tail
Contentedness of a cat's purr
Happy laughter that reaches the eyes
Precious time spent with loved ones
Reunions
Being home
A restful sleep
That first sip of coffee
Opening a real newspaper
Breakfast for dinner
A celebratory, festive flute of bubbly.
(Even better with a strawberry.)
An iced-cold beer on a hot summer evening
Anticipation (better than sudden surprises)
Musical theatre
Popcorn movies
Baseball stadiums
Family adventures
Music...lots and lots of music
The one bright moment of the day-- the
kind word, the reassuring hug, or the
silent prayer that made it worthwhile

I *especially* love the sunflower

~ RED RIBBON ~

One of my favorite possessions is a pair of Wiss® scissors that my mom passed down to me years ago. She said they were the best ones she ever had. She had fastened a little piece of red yarn ribbon to the grip of the scissors. The bright red yarn had allowed her to spot them among her piles of pens, pencils, letter openers and other notions.

After some 50-odd years, the red ribbon is frayed and worn, but there it remains on the scissors.

The other day as I was cutting some paper with these scissors, my husband noticed that the ribbon had thinned quite a bit, and it was coming loose. He asked to take hold of the scissors, and then proceeded to salvage what was left of the loose scraps of yarn by carefully tying the frayed ribbon into a neat little bow around the handle. I was moved by his seemingly small, but significant attention to detail.

As I watched him working, it occurred to me that this pair of scissors is one of the few tangible gifts from my mom that I still have, which is why the scissors mean so much to me. They mean more to me now. They still work like a charm, but the best thing about them is the red accessory Mom placed there some 50-odd years ago for a purely functional purpose. Every time I use the scissors, I'm reminded of her practical side. And I'm nostalgic for it.

March

~ *Honking* ~

Your honking is an imperfection
When I stop at an intersection.

To block it is against the law;
Plus, traffic's moving at a crawl.

My first reaction when you honk?
I check both sides of the crosswalk,

And make sure bikes upon my right
Are trav'ling well within my sight.

Your honking doesn't make me hurry --
Instead, I'll pause without a worry

So thank you for your kind concern
But really -- next time, wait your turn.

~ Lemons ~

Sometimes when the day's been long,
we're tired or anxious; unaware,
The slightest unkind contradiction
makes collective tempers flare.
Words supporting strangers and that treat
the loved one like she's wrong
Or argumentative retorts for minor
slights make evenings long.

Yet when I try to make things right, or
say you didn't have to chide,
Your sudden silent, cold retreat is
something that I can't abide.
True, life will throw us sour curves,
but let's avoid the harsh tirade.
Why can't we take our lemons and
return the gift with lemonade?

~ *The Neighborhood* ~

Not so long ago this was an isolated land
Visitors avoided it; they didn't understand.
Speaking of our neighborhood, they'd
laugh that we'd been fooled
Locals didn't mind because we knew the hills were gold.

"It's Seattle's best-kept secret," folks
would murmur with a wink.
"The honeymoon would end if city planners found a link."
But find a link they did, and placed
a high bridge o'er the bay.
Visitors no longer laugh about it – but they stay.

Detours will direct them to a most enchanting beach,
A little slice of paradise within convenient reach.
They'll watch the passing ferry
boats when taking in a run
Or gaze at the Olympics underneath a setting sun.

Culture and fine arts ensure folks won't depart in haste.
Cafes, pubs and restaurant fare
enhance both mood and taste.
The city's oldest neighborhood is
younger than its years –
This gem? It's West Seattle. That's
like music to my ears.

~ A Touch of Class ~

It may lack rhythm
But it has heart
If I had gone back
And perfected it
To suit your tastes
I would have removed the heart from it
That I tried so hard to put there.
If I'd given it rhythm, and tempo,
And beat, and form,
It would have had no meaning
Because it would not have been me.
True, I'm a little offbeat and off-color –
And very imperfect. But I like it that way.
If you want things in me that are not me,
Then you must not want me at all, but someone else.
Someone who may look like me, dress like me,
Talk like me.
But not me.
Because you do not want what is in my heart for you.

~ *Willie, I Understand* ~

To all the men I've loved before
The first was cute, but nothing more
The second was a selfish boor
The third was unemployed and poor

To all the men I've cared about
The fourth, a narcissistic lout
The fifth, I really have no doubt
Was nothing to write home about

To all the men I've ever known
The sixth was just the seventh's clone
The eighth was faithless to the bone
The ninth would not leave me alone

To all the men I ever knew
The tenth man fled to Timbuktu
He sent a card – with postage due
Eleven fell for number two

The twelfth was stoned; the thirteenth drunk
The fourteenth thought he was a hunk
The fifteenth liked new wave and punk
The sixteenth's sense of humor stunk

I've lost them all! I should be glad
It's funny, but it's kind of sad
And seventeen may not be bad
But he won't be the ones I've had.

April

~ *Because It Is* ~

*Another mini-poem (without any
tedious rhyming this time)*

Love those days …
where there is a lifting of the spirit;
where your heart soars for no apparent reason
other than that you dreamt a good dream and
woke up to the shining sun
ready to greet a brand-new day
filled with promise and hope.

I wish to have faith in my dreams;
To live honorably with no regrets;
To love wisely, laugh loudly, and
listen intently.
I will practice patience and
be kind to myself and others.

Believe and rejoice in Goodness, because life is a good
thing.
Put aside sorrow, regret and resentment.
Life is funny. Exercise those laugh lines.
Don't regret what you've done, because it's done. It's
behind you now.
Don't regret what you haven't done. Your future awaits you.
Don't regret what you can't control. Let it go.
Celebrate your plethora of choices instead of blaming
them.

Replenish. Give. Live!
Treat each moment with dignity and reverence.
Stop putting faith -- or worse, doubt -- in your tomorrows.
Live for today, for God's sake.
Respect each experience in your day as if this is the one
that counts.

~ *The Mockingbird* ~

Mom took us to the movies on a Friday night
We bought our popcorn, found our seats
The lights dimmed and the search beam flashed its welcome light
Excitedly, we munched on sweets

The film was from a book, "To Kill a Mockingbird."
('Twas black-and-white, but what the heck)
I thought it was about some misbehaving kids
Until I saw that Mr. Peck.

Commanded quite a presence, but the kind of dad
-- Made parenthood look like a cinch
He was a lawyer, but he was an honest man
Named Atticus, the last name Finch.

It was a tragic tale, but heart-rending, too
Of prejudice, how it's unfair
We learn to love, but we can also learn to hate
And justice can be all too rare.

Atticus was gentle, kind and very strong
He stood for goodness and for right
But fear can sometimes grab and hold folks in its grips
False testimony "won" that fight.

The kids were keen observers, but until that day
They'd feared a neighbor who'd been kind
When they came home they found some gifts awaiting them
And after that, they weren't so blind.

I'd always gone to movies to be entertained
But thanks to writer Harper Lee,
It's possible to laugh but cry and learn some too,
Behind the cinema's marquee.

~ *The One in the Window* ~

First, there's the moment when she says yes
Then comes the day that she chooses a dress,
Makes color selections and rounds out a theme.
The venue's reserved. Soon, it's all like a dream ~~
The day is approaching, their wedding's in June,
They hire a DJ; decide a dance tune.
She checks off the guest list (the
loved ones they'll greet!)
Yet soon, she discovers she's getting cold feet.
She questions her judgment one meaningful night;
Inspecting her gown, she knows something's not right.
Before long, it nags her.
She'll wonder.
She'll pray ~~
And decides she'll confront it one ominous day.
Supplies have been ordered; invites have gone out
So, why is she suddenly harboring doubt??
Her mind knows it's rash, but her heart says she should.
Her sister supports her, and friends say it's good.
So, a sequined and pearly gown within reach
Replaces the <u>first</u> one she bought, which was peach.
With that final moment, she vowed to say yes
to the one in the window ~~ the perfect new dress.

~ *The Piano* ~

The piano is dusty and hasn't been played for years
The water spots on it resemble a person's tears

The aroma is ancient and musty, but hardly a reek
The beautiful wood makes it obvious it's an antique

I wonder whose hands have once
graced the vanilla-stained keys
I query whose craftsmanship
fashioned what everyone sees

My fingers touch lightly – but Oh!
How they sound like a prayer
If it wasn't before, Holy Providence surely is there

This magic invention makes poets of women and men
The piano has found a new home
and she'll sing once again.

~ *Unconquered II* ~

*(with thanks to William Ernest Henley, 1849-1903,
and to my daughter Emily for her
positive inspiration and love)*

In spite of the spite that hovers here,
Dark as the moon on moonless nights,
I'm grateful that Spirit guides my way
And leads me to ever-burning lights.

It isn't that I don't gripe or cry
Or pity myself on darker days
It's just that I keep my head held high
And continue to follow the warm sun's blaze.

I face the future with new resolve
To be a good person; to face my fears,
Enthusiastically learning more
And confronting each setback that appears.

It matters not that I've felt betrayed
By promises that were thrust apart
I am the one inside my head;
The permanent keeper of my heart.

~ *Waiting* ~

Woke up out of sorts; my head was jarred
Nothing's wrong but I've been on my guard
I see the mailman right outside my yard
And realize the waiting is what's hard

Seems these days there's really no excuse
Shall I put up with this self-abuse?
You know my number, and you have a cell
Yet here I'm sitting, sounding like Adele

Our latest conversation was just fine
I didn't see a clue or any sign
So, even though I can't claim you as mine,
You could at least have offered me a line

At risk of sounding like that rhyming Bard
Or something less than my last greeting card
My image of you's permanently marred
The waiting didn't have to be this hard

<u>May</u>

~ *Emily* ~

You touched your sock and then you smiled
When I said "sock" today
We're starting to communicate
In such a subtle way

My most enchanting moment was
When I gave birth to you
Your father witnessed everything
So magical and new

And now you're running, climbing and
You laugh with dancing eyes
You're such a little innocent
Yet bright and fun and wise

You look like such an angel when
You're sleeping in your bed
The Lord made you his gift to us
Soon after we were wed

A sweeter little treasure, I
Don't think we'll ever see
My dear, we're yours forever – and
We're called a family.

~ HIS NAME WAS ROBERT ~

My love of reading came from both of my parents, but mostly from my dad. Mom instilled in me a passion for the performing arts and the artists who brought them to life, both in front of and behind the scenes. My dad is the reason I write. Not only did he drag home hefty piles of library books for me to read, he challenged and inspired me to write my own stories and, later, a lot of poems.

Dad brought home the entire Mary Poppins book series by P.L. Travers. He also introduced me to the Oz series of books. It amazed me to learn that the movies that resulted were inspired by an entire series of books, rather than just one. If those series were written today, they would probably launch a half-dozen movies apiece. I very much doubt that any of them would match the magic of the original *Wizard of Oz* and *Mary Poppins* motion pictures. They are both irreplaceable classics.

In this manner, my dad also taught me to appreciate movies. I treated him to a movie for the first time when I was 17 years old; it was my first R-rated movie. (It cost 50 cents a ticket at a second-run movie house.) The movie was *The Godfather.* My mom passed on it, but my brother and one of my sisters joined my dad and me on our movie outing. It was an intense film experience, and we all loved seeing it together. My sister was taken with Al Pacino, previously unknown to us, and I developed the hots for James Caan. But we were all impressed with Al Pacino's acting and expected big things out of him. (We weren't disappointed.)

This experience was especially memorable because it was the last movie I saw at a theater with my dad. He passed away the following May.

Dad taught me to love so many things, but most of all, he instilled in me a love and respect for the male of the species that I appreciate to this day. He was, like most girls' dads, the first man in my life and the man against whom I naturally compared all others. Very, very hard shoes for anyone to fill -- but I instinctively knew that the man I ended up marrying would have loved him as much as I did. That realization was when I knew I'd met the right guy.

~ *Missing a Friend* ~

A cool designer outfit,
A new and stylish 'do
A shiny carwash, awesome meal,
The gift of something new

Accomplishment at work or sports
A challenge tried and met
A fascinating, fun pursuit
The payment of a debt

A quick and happy laugh out loud
A sudden raise in pay
An evening out with an old friend
A really special day

Are all marred by your absence
Not knowing how you are
Not seeing you, not even sure
You're driving the same car

Lately there's an empty space
You used to occupy
Not my intention to disturb,
Just wish that I knew why.

~ *Motherhood* ~

Motherhood is the best, and the hardest, endeavor there is.
It's the best, because your heart swells with joy whenever you're with your little ones.
There's nothing in the world like seeing her take her first step and witnessing her discovery of newfound independence,
Or receiving a spontaneous hug from your son when you hand him a balloon,
Or when she asks for a story at bedtime -- not one of the stories you usually read, but one of your own from when you were young, and the happy memories are shared once more.
Proudly watching as he helps Dad with the groceries, or laughing out loud as he enthusiastically tells a funny joke;
Attending her first tap-dancing recital, and later seeing her step onstage in a play, wowing the audience (and you) with her sweetness and grace;
Hearing him plunk a familiar tune on the piano with ease,
And so it goes.

The hardest is when your child cries
And you're unable to provide consolation because you're not yet sure what's wrong
Or later, when she comes home from school, feeling sad that she has "no friends"
Or when he gets into trouble for something he didn't know was wrong
Maybe even something I taught him to do
When she feels excluded from playdates
When he struggles at school

When she starts to wear makeup and you feel her slipping
away
When he starts to watch shows about zombies and insists
you watch with him
(And you start to like them but can't explain why!)
Anyway, you get my point.

One day you wake up, feeling both proud and prematurely
sentimental
As you watch her prepare to graduate from high school;
Or wait for him to walk down the aisle, crying tears of joy
for his happy accomplishment.
One day soon afterward, much too soon, when your
children decide -- one by one -- to experience life on
their own
Without you there to guide them, to hold hands with them,
or to keep them safe,
And you realize you've learned every bit as much from
them as you've taught them?
That's the best feeling in the world – and also the hardest.

~ *Seventeen, for My Daughter* ~

Sinatra spoke of 17
and called it a good year
But I was fully 12 months shy
of having my first beer

I got my driver's license
but I didn't have a car
And rode my bike where're I went
but never got too far

Became a senior that fine year
but missed out on my prom
(One girl went a bit too far
and she came back a mom)

I did go out with one nice boy
it somehow didn't click
Considered all my college options
none of which would stick

Ah! 17's still innocent
and fancy-free, you see
And it will be another year
before "legality"

Life can sometimes hit you
square and hard between the eyes
But Emily, you are --- beyond
your years --- so very wise

So live and learn and laugh with joy
'cuz 17 moves fast
What makes our greatest moments great
is that they cannot last

And know this is a stepping-stone,
a launching pad between
Your golden and enchanted youth
and when you turn 18.

To my beautiful, precious daughter Emily,
With Love from Mom

~ *You Look Good on Paper* ~

Was called in for my year's review
I thought it would be mild
And hoped like heck I'd get my raise
Because I was with child.

He sat me down in front of him
(I felt the cushion taper)
He shook his head and then he said,
"Well, you look good – on paper."

He ventured that he couldn't put
His finger on the issue
"But there are problems with the fit,"
He smugly said, with tissue.

I turned the tissue down – no, thanks! –
(My dignity's my saber)
But I was stunned and once at home,
Went promptly into labor.

I swore when I returned to work
My will would be like steel
I'd tell them that the "shoe" fits fine –
But my boss is a heel.

It didn't matter 'cuz he quit
But here's one thing I learned:
Looking good on paper doesn't
Mean you won't get burned.

June

~ *Hotel Colorado* ~

We booked a stay at Hotel Colorado
On a visit to the town of Glenwood Springs
The bridal suite was rumored to be haunted
With some nutty paranormal happenings

The room itself had quite a reputation
For housing well-known guests like Al Capone
We thought it might be fun to see this showpiece
But weren't too fond to venture there alone

My spouse and I were visiting our family
And stayed there with the kids one summer night
The room assigned us was the bridal chamber
The decor, overpoweringly white

It looked (and reeked) as sterile as a psych ward...
(This, conveniently omitted by our hosts)
Yet, though we spent a somewhat sleepless night there
We failed to encounter any ghosts

At daylight, we had breakfast in their cafe
And heard more scary, creepy tales of doom
But, concluding that the spirits were on our side,
Spent a peaceful second night in that same room

Although we didn't witness apparitions
This ending's not as jolly as it seems:
We saw no ghost inhabitants in person
But since then, they've invaded countless dreams.

~ THE MEANING OF GRATITUDE ~

From 2002

My sister Mara died in July 2000 after a long illness. I am just now beginning to come to terms with it through the grace of God and the support of many wonderful people. Although our family laughed often, much of Mara's life was sad. After she died, my niece Tesa asked us to share our favorite memories about her. She wanted happy Mara stories. This is one of mine.

Mara graduated from high school one year before I completed eighth grade at a parochial school. At Mara's high school, the students were involved in an annual fundraiser. They were to go door-to-door to sell holly, garlands and other Christmas greens. If they sold a certain amount, they would earn a school "holly-day." Although Mara had always sold her quota, she was not in the mood for it her senior year. She jokingly asked me to do it for her. To be trusted with such an important task was irresistible to me. Long story short, Mara earned her day off. She earnestly stated that if I ever needed a big favor, to just ask.

The following year, each student in my eighth-grade class was assigned the task of submitting a valedictory essay for a school assembly. The instructor would select five students to read their essays at the Baccalaureate ceremony at the end of the school year. My usually active creative juices froze. Not knowing where to start, I went home and asked Mara if she had any ideas. She said she would think about it and get back to me.

The next day, I was flabbergasted when she came to me with a completed essay! It was beautifully written; I did not change a single word. I felt a little guilty about it, but Mara said to accept it as a gift, as she had been waiting for the opportunity to do something for me. My assignment completed, I proudly brought it to school and recited it to the class.

The five students were selected for both content and presentation. I was a would-be actress who enjoyed an audience, so the presentation was no problem for me. But it was the content of Mara's essay that won me a slot. Everyone said it was the best-*written* speech in the entire class.

Obviously, I felt conflicted. I went home and told Mara and the rest of the family what had happened. They all thought it was great – especially Mara, who was extremely flattered I'd won. I told her I felt awkward taking credit for a speech I had not written. In her fervent, loving way, Mara said she would make it easy for me. She forbade me from telling my teacher or anyone else at school that she wrote the essay. It was her gift to me, she said, and I should accept it fully, without guilt, and anyway, that what you do with a gift you receive is none of the giver's business. I've never forgotten that.

As far as Mara was concerned, the fact that the essay was one of the five selected for presentation was pretty much the whole point. It was as if she knew. At the much-awaited (and somewhat dreaded) Baccalaureate ceremony, I stood on that stage and proudly read the essay. Sure enough, everyone loved it. They were moved by it, but no one more than I as I read it. I'll never forget Mara's unselfish act, nor the pride I felt toward my family that day.

The essay itself was about Gratitude; that we should be thankful for the many things we take for granted every day. Wow. If anyone knew the meaning of Gratitude, it was Mara. Just for selling a measly 25 bucks' worth of Christmas greens, she gave me some of the most treasured gifts I've ever been given – her love, her thanks, her trust, her kindness, and her conspiratorial sense of humor – all wrapped up in a beautiful, brilliant and succinct piece of writing. For this and many other reasons she lives forever in my heart.

~ Simple Rules for Overseas Travel ~

If you have the means to go, here's some of what you'll need to know:

- Pack some shirts and pairs of pants.
- Get your passport in advance.
- For reading on the long plane ride, bring a Rick Steves travel guide.
- Don't forget a prepaid phone.
- Keep track of every separate zone.
- Euros are the currencies for many overseas countries.
- If you need a pound or frank, then seek an ATM or bank.
- Travel light with just one bag –

  - Bring Ibuprofen for jet lag;
  - A change of lingerie each day;
  - A fanny pack to tuck away;
  - *Quick Guide* for foreign-language sites;
  - An appetite for local bites.

Once you're there, relax and rest. Enjoy a shower and get dressed.
Then take good photos; see a show; stop and have a cup of joe.
Enjoy the ambiance and mood, and bring an open attitude.

Make sure to shop for souvenirs before your flight's departure nears.
Otherwise, you'll spend a lot and may not like the gifts you got.
A journal that you wrote in well should work back home for show-and-tell.

It was a lot of money spent, but (Man, oh Man!) how well it went.
When it's all over, don't be sad – think back on all the fun you had.
Then, on some lazy afternoon, plan next year's trip – and take it soon.

~ *TO YOU, FROM ME* ~

Theatre has been a part of my life from the time I was four years old and was bitten by the stage bug on a family trip to Hawaii. Once you take the stage and experience the applause, the laughter, and the positive vibes that follow, you're hooked. I discovered that my love affair with the stage didn't stop at the footlights. I was equally fond of the process, which included working on stage crews; as an usher; in the lighting booth; as an assistant stage manager and stage manager; and eventually as a playwright, director and executive producer.

You know all this, which is why you and I got off to a good start almost immediately. We met in the best of all possible times, under the most ideal of circumstances: backstage during *Evita*. It was the first and only extension of a production in Seattle's Civic Light Opera history. Even though we hardly knew each other, I admired your initiative and sense of responsibility from the beginning. You were both serious and good-humored. And even though you had a two-hour one-way commute, you showed up at lots of cast parties. I began to notice that you always sat at my table.

During the following production, a favorite of mine – *My Fair Lady* – you had the backstage crew laughing and joking. By the third show, The *Oxydol Hour*, several of us were vying for your affections.

More productions followed: *A Funny Thing Happened On the Way To the Forum*; *My One and Only*; *Brigadoon*; *Into The Woods*; *Man of La Mancha*; *Pajama Game*; *On Your Toes*; *Wonderful Town*; *Hair*; *Texas Chainsaw*

Manicurist; and many, many more. (These are listed in memory order; not necessarily chronological order.)

During a much-needed production break, your subtle attention toward me became apparent (to me, anyway). Before long, we were an item. Warm, caring, thoughtful and fair, yet consistently true to your values, you were and are always there for me. Even when we don't agree on things, you don't turn your back on an argument -- although half the time, I'm the one who started it.

You accept and appreciate my treasured friends. You love my family not necessarily because they *are* lovable – and they are – but because they are mine. You never take me to a movie I don't want to see. It's amazing to me that although I felt complete without you, I feel so much more complete with you. It would be like setting *Pygmalion* to music... (oh wait, that's already happened).

For the last three-plus years we've shared each other's thoughts, prayers and dreams, sometimes without even knowing it. After today, we'll share each other's bank accounts and income tax filings. What a romantic thought! At times during the last seven months of preparing for this day, I wished we had just gone ahead and eloped. But now, I'm glad we didn't. If anything prepares you for marriage, it's an engagement period. The decisions, the compromises, the spending, the organizing, and the constant awareness that this is forever and that it's for love really make you think.

I love you. You are my best friend. Borrowing from the playwright N. Richard Nash, who scripted *The Rainmaker*, today I finally know how it feels to say the word "husband." It feels good.

~ *Venus de Milo* ~

"So, that's what wrong with you," he laughed,
responding to my status as a late bloomer.
Was it somehow wrong to discover
romantic love late in life?
We all love differently, and in varying degrees,
rendering mutual, rapturous and permanent love
as rare and precious as catching a falling star.
Why are affairs of the heart so elusive?

Perhaps the answer lies with Venus – Love personified
in a statue that depicts the epitome of graceful female beauty.
We are inexplicably drawn to this mystical, sensuous figure;
an image so lovely, yet so obviously damaged,
that to appreciate her
means to graciously accept the flaw without overlooking it
and to recognize, in seeing her exactly as she is,
that we are in the very presence of greatness.

This is Love in its purest and truest form –
accepting and appreciating, laughing and admiring,
and catching – even embracing – the myriad flaws
without knowing why, without understanding,
without questioning, without meddling.
Just happily, effortlessly returning the Love she gives freely.
Would that we could be this forgiving
with our flesh-and-blood counterparts.

That's what's wrong with us: although graceful,
strong, kind, lovely, handsome, smart, rich, or talented,
in Love, we become unrecognizable –
immodestly, rapturously throwing caution to the wind
yet prudishly, desperately refusing to shed our inner,
private selves
in search of a perfection that doesn't exist.
The irony is that to forfeit imperfect love
with all its splendid, irrational, and irritating contradictions
renders us lifeless.

Despite the pain, the mystery, and the misery,
the only cure is to love
with decency, with kindness, and without moral compromise,
and to understand that to truly experience Love
is to move us, like Venus herself, one step closer
to the warmth and power of Earth's closest star.

July

~ BETTE AND FAYE ~

My humble claim to fame is that I'm three degrees from Kevin Bacon – and it's all because of a TV movie called *The Disappearance of Aimee*, starring Faye Dunaway. Faye Dunaway starred in *Chinatown* with Jack Nicholson, and Jack Nicholson was in *A Few Good Men* with Kevin Bacon.

The Disappearance of Aimee takes place in 1920s Los Angeles. The TV movie was filmed in Denver, Colorado in the sweltering summer of 1976. A friend of mine who was working on the shoot asked if I'd like to appear in a few scenes as one of many faces in a crowded congregation of drab mourners dressed in black. "Sure," I quipped, "it sounds like fun." But as a movie buff, I jumped at the opportunity.

Our scene was shot in a large old building that doubled as a community center where church services were held. The idea was for the group of extras to blend in as part of the scenery, apparently to keep from upstaging the stars of the show: The striking diva Faye Dunaway, and that aging actress of campy 1960s horror films, Bette Davis.

I couldn't wait to catch a glimpse of my idol, Faye Dunaway, a movie star in the prime of her career. Bette Davis, on the other hand, could best be described as morbidly fascinating. It's not that I considered her an unappealing has-been or anything. No, she was far worse -- freakish and scary. Casting directors frequently tapped her to play ghoulish characters in movies like *Whatever Happened to Baby Jane?* and *Hush, Hush Sweet Charlotte*. In person I imagined her to be cold, aloof and a bit frightening.

The extras arrived early on the day of the shoot, and we waited for the scene to start. Several hours passed while we talked, snacked, fanned ourselves furiously, and proceeded to grow restless in our seats. During our wait, Faye Dunaway's assistant emerged to explain that the delay was due to a wardrobe problem. Meanwhile, Bette Davis stood by and mingled with musicians and members of the tech crew.

A while later with no fanfare, no introduction, and still no Ms. Dunaway, Bette Davis walked onto the stage and approached the center pulpit. Her hair was done up in curlers, which didn't diminish the sudden panic I felt. It was a surreal and spooky moment. The room grew so quiet that you could hear a pin drop.

The silence was shattered a moment later by the click and flash of a camera from somewhere in the congregation. Surprised, Ms. Davis backed up for a second - and then she spoke directly to the mortified picture-taker with mock indignity. There was embarrassed laughter from a few folks in the congregation, but I just smiled. I wouldn't have wanted *my* picture snapped wearing curlers, either!

I half expected her to storm offstage after that. Instead, looking calm and composed, she smiled warmly as her eyes scanned the crowd. She produced a book, opened it and began to read to us in a clear, loud voice. Ms. Davis was a remarkable storyteller – fun, witty and thoroughly captivating. She occasionally interjected a poignant or funny little aside, and engaged the extras in some light banter. She even directed us in singing an old, familiar song, and enlisted a musician to accompany us on the organ. All the while, she kept an eye on the film crew for signals of readiness.

Ever resourceful, Bette Davis had recognized a need and had bravely stepped in to fill it (curlers and all). From that point forward, the afternoon proceeded pleasantly and easily. Ms. Davis won my admiration and my heart, and I became a lifelong fan of hers. Even better, I still enjoy Faye Dunaway as an actress. Her "disappearance" over a costume snafu didn't impress her many fans, but the day's events did humanize her. Although no longer my idol, she became something even better: relatable.

All in all, *The Disappearance of Aimee* was a grand experience, with the fun little bonus of placing me three precious degrees from Kevin Bacon.

~ *Kahlua* ~

Only a week ago Kitty was here
We loved her a lot; she was wild and dear
But suddenly Sunday she didn't return
By Monday, I started to voice my concern

We checked with the neighbors; called Feline Control
We put "Missing Kitty" signs on every pole
And although a week isn't too long a wait,
We still are uncertain of Little One's fate.

One other thing that really makes it a drag:
She recently lost her flea collar and tag
They say that a cat's something you cannot tame
But I miss her, and wonder if I am to blame

My toddler keeps asking me, "Mama, where's Klaw?"
Can I explain it to someone so small?
My daughter will hopefully, quickly forget
But I'll always remember this wonderful pet.

~ *The Lady* ~

The faded beauty stands alone, aloft; but not aloof
Her long, wavy hair
Pulled to one side
Wearing an unmistakably recognizable headpiece
Her royal, sophisticated bearing in sharp contrast
To an approachable warmth
Unique -- yet common is she
With her uncovered feet and her loose green covering
That appears more suited for slumber
than for the outdoors
An unassuming and lovely sight
Welcoming the huddled masses
With a promise of shelter and new beginnings
She holds a well-lit torch high above her head
Regal and earnest, yet relaxed and calm
A tablet placed in her left hand with
the year of liberty's birth
Beckoning, inviting; delivering kindness,
Inspiring hope,
And exuding love.

~ Really? ~

Do things sometimes not make sense?
Do you feel unease and distrust
Even toward the people you trust the most?
Do you experience some creeping paranoia
Like everyone's out to get you
Or they simply consider you irrelevant?

The part you're cast in is minor
But key – you need to be there
Because your absence would be noticed
Not because you are you, mind you,
But because of the role you play.
You could be anybody. You just happen to be Mom.

~ Weren't it better When the Mob Ran Vegas ~

We're taking a ride from a shuttle driver
We're leaving behind the famous City of Sin
We're sitting there; the driver turns a corner
And decides he's gonna let us in
He says, "yes, sirree, this town sure is different
Yes, sirree, things certainly have changed
They've gotten rid of quite a few old places
Everything's been rearranged...
The Mafia, way back when, owned this-here city
Served cheap meals and booze to suck you in
They'd bring in lots of free, live entertainment
Pay their cronies with some shots of gin."

Weren't it better when the Mob ran Vegas
Weren't things richer when they had their way
Not that I would want to be a member
But please don't tell me crime don't pay

(He went on) "Then, the town was in the Mob's back pockets
Now, they've cleaned it out and look what's left
The corporate underground has taken over
They're robbing us with every cent
Big business runs the place and makes big money
All the good ol' stuff has been replaced
Casinos here are now a dime a dozen
Pay more money, see a lot more waste."

Weren't it better when the Mob ran Vegas
Weren't things richer when they had their way
Not that I would want to be a member
But please don't tell me crime don't pay

I asked the driver if he lived in Vegas
He said, "well, sure, 'cuz flashiness still sells
Folks like me still come to play the Bandits
Stay in fancy, colorful hotels."
I said, "well, I'm not really into gambling."
He said, "well, truth to tell, that don't mean Jack!
Gamblin's legal pretty much all over
That don't mean the business has your back."

Weren't it better when the Mob ran Vegas
Heck, I can gamble just a mile away
Why hop a plane and buy expensive liquor
When I don't even like to play??
And please -- don't tell me crime don't pay!

August

~ *August Moon* ~

Seems yesterday we gave "high-fives"
To mark the start of June
Today we're buying school supplies
Beneath an August moon.

It's sunny still, but not for long
The days are moving fast
And final remnants of free time
Are quickly flying past.

The first new day of school,
So full of promise, will be here
We'll meet new teachers, greet old friends,
Embrace another year

While thinking back on how the summer
Ended all too soon
And with a wistful, fond farewell,
We'll bless the August moon.

~ Kitch ~

The wild horse on August 4th
Was sole witness to a mass murder
Involving the extortion of thousands of dollars
Hidden in a secret bank vault in the country.
A modern farm house with an old man to care for him
He owned his own dentist's chair and equipment
But he had bad teeth his whole life
A secret passageway to this house led to a
children's theatre space and museum
Where I had played Snow White when I was 23
Yet my fondest memory of the museum
Relates to the young man who gave
me my first tour of the place
Another passageway led to a huge arena
Where, presently, a circus is being performed
Dromedaries are walking by the passageway
And hear my footsteps.

A separate small building leads to the bank vault,
Which is halfway submerged in water at this time.
It was here where the mysterious mass murder occurred --
A murder that only the bronze wild horse saw.
Since that fateful evening at eleven-ten pm
He refuses to be ridden, or even touched.
The old man has since passed away
The farmhouse all but abandoned
And the story is relayed by a young lad
Who could not possibly have been old enough
To have been born when the tragic event occurred
An event that disrupted this quiet little area of town
Forever.

A blue horse with white "socks" around its legs
And a white streak running down its forehead
Appears with a colt who is the spitting image of him.
The lad runs into the farmhouse to inform the wild horse.
"Kitch!" he cries. "Kitch! Kitch!"
The wild horse rears; looks startled
Kitch is his name
And the only word to which he responds.
I look at the horse sadly
And realize in that instant
That I will tame him – and train him
Yet his wild spirit will always remain.

~ *Latitude Attitude* ~

The heat of a sweltering summer day
The careless loss of a favorite glove
The shaking hand from a shattered glass
The pain of an unrequited love...

The sweet contentment of faith renewed
The cheerful laughter of children's play
The catchy sound of a favorite tune
The heat of a welcome summer day...

~ *My Cat* ~

I had to give my cat away
He was but six months old
My landlord said I couldn't keep him
Why was he so cold?

Perhaps a kind heart rescued him
Before he was put down
I'll never know -- but thoughts of him
Cause me to weep and frown.

~ There Used to Be a Fish Called Salmon ~

When I was your age, my mom would serve us frozen salmon with rice.
She was a wonderful cook, but there was something *about*
The seafood caught in Denver, Colorado –
It hurt my teeth to chew it and I thought it tasted funny.
Years later, though, after I moved to the coast of Puget Sound
(And the braces were removed from my teeth)
Salmon became my favorite seafood.
The color of the meat was so unusual that its name *was*
its color.
It was sort of a coral-pink, with scales like sterling.

The Chinook was the King of the Sea: when it was baked
to perfection
Adding a bit of wine, garlic, dill and butter,
And served with all the right accompaniments –
Wild rice, warm sourdough, Caesar salad, asparagus with
cheese sauce
And, of course, a favorite wine – it was a meal made in
culinary Heaven.
The salmon melted in your mouth, it was so tender and flaky.
The composition of the fish was fascinating, too;
Like flat row houses you could peel away
One by one, and savor each succulent morsel individually.
This seafood didn't need tartar or lemon.
I'd go so far as to say that if I could have only one more meal
On this earth before I died,
It would be salmon.

Things have changed a lot over the years –
in many ways, for the better.
And still, some memories are irreplaceable
Like lounging on the old porch swing
And sipping fresh cold lemonade with my siblings;
Playing hide-and-go-seek with the neighbors until dark;
Or the ting-a-ling chime of Mom's brass dinner bell
That happily signaled suppertime.
But of all the things I once enjoyed that are gone,
I would never have imagined that you'd hear me say
There used to be a fish
Called salmon.

September

~ *The Entertainer* ~

*Written for and dedicated to Thomas
with love and appreciation.*

His eyes were on mine from the first moment
And they laughed.
Not to make fun, although he loves to have fun,
But because he knew me.
Just like that.
He knows my soul without words
And he, though impetuous, is kind.

"What should I be when I grow up?"
He asked me one day.
"A writer, a builder,
Someone who makes art?"
He likes limericks, Legos and
letting loose with his drawings.
"Maybe," I said.
"Or," he pondered, "maybe I'll become a priest."
He still loves the light-hearted Bible book
One of his aunts gave him
for his First Holy Communion.

He's beautiful and handsome and
Wouldn't want to admit it,
but he's cute, too.
He cracks up the kids in class
and sometimes, his teachers.
He's easily remembered
by people whose names escape us.

He lights up a room with his funny jokes.
He carries a tune like he was born to it,
And he plays the piano with eloquence and skill.
You wouldn't know it
Because he's still a boy
(Cranky and occasionally exasperating)
But give him a few years
To hone his God-given gifts
And he'll delight the world
Like he delights me now.

~ *Once A Dancer* ~

The windows are partially boarded on the
old downtown brownstone hotel.
She sits inside eating soggy corn flakes,
drinking lukewarm Sanka,
And watching *Lucy* reruns on a twelve-
inch black-&-white television screen.
The dingy white window curtain only partially obscures
Her view of the ugly world outside
But passersby can see her sitting at
that kitchen table and chair
With a shower cap over her head to hide
the fact that she's lost her hair
And they, momentarily ashamed, turn away from her.

She had been young and pretty once
and she used to *love* to dance!
The men noticed her with her red silk
gowns and cascading blonde hair.
She was desirable but aloof
And, in spite of a wide assortment of
suitors, chose never to marry.

She had dreams of becoming an architect,
but with no formal education
Instead became the dancer she knew she could be.
She had natural talent and sensual charm
And worked wherever there was money.
As the years passed and she slowly
lost her looks and figure
The jobs faded and men no longer took an interest in her.

She sits today, almost oblivious to the fact
That this hotel that, in another
world, she could have built
Is scheduled for demolition. She is not really unaware –
She has just stopped caring about what will happen.

Soon, she will carry all of her meager
belongings in a couple of Hefty sacks
And she'll join the passersby on the outside
of the new high-rise condominium
On the spot that she used to facetiously
call home. She doesn't think
Much about her predicament because
it has become her reality.
Her only goals are to see the sun rise and
to ignore the curious, frightened
And hateful looks that total strangers give her.
She owes the ugly world no explanations –
she has every right to be here.
She's a woman for the ages.
She's a dancer.

~ *September Born* ~

For Tricia

Don't ask why certain things happen in our lives
That bring us to certain places
All I know is, you were there so many times at just the right moment.
I'm blessed with everything I need and more
And am not one to reach out easily to others
But prefer to watch from afar, listen and observe.
YET – once in a while – I connect.
Like a leech.

And then it becomes hard – maybe even impossible – for me to detach.
Remember Red Robin in downtown Seattle?
On a warm summer night, while enjoying happy hour with colleagues,
Something you said to a mutual friend was so right-on; it was so thoughtful, so kind, so funny (too bad I don't recall what it was)
That I felt I got you right away
And that you just might get me too, once you got to know me.
Dear friend, I had *no* idea!

It's literally taken me this long to realize
That our dearest friends are a part of ourselves.
They comprise so much of who we are, who we become, and
Who we were meant to be.
We're so, so different, you and I
Yet no matter where I am or what I do,
You're always there with me.

This September day is a blessing to your loved ones,
A cause for joyous wining, dining, revelry,
music, laughter, enchantment...
Basically, everything that's good and happy in this life.
This is your gift.
Your birthday itself has become something precious to me.
May this celebration to honor it exceed your hopes and
dreams
And may it become, for a lifetime of tomorrows, a treasured
memory.

~ *Seventeen, for My Son* ~

Sinatra spoke of 17
and called it a good year?
You can't vote, marry, get tattoos,
Or legally drink beer

You can get a driver's license
But you still won't have a car
You'll ride the bus or take your bike
Yet may not get too far.

Like you, I was a junior
It was met with dignity
(But nothing as impressive as
Your project on Bruce Lee).

I managed to play basketball;
It somehow didn't click
Considered all my college options,
None of which would stick.

See, 17's still innocent
But challenges await
Like when the t.v. season starts
Or going on a date.

Thomas, life is funny --
Even scary; sometimes sly
But your keen, insightful nature
Future years will dignify.

So live and learn and keep the faith
'cuz 17 moves fast
Your teenage years are worth so much,
Because they never last.

Enjoy each day and heed these words
Ignore them at your peril
Or someday you may end up like
The zombie bro of Daryl.

Of 17, one thing holds true
In Jersey or Japan
This is the year that, when it's through,
You'll launch from lad to man.

To my smart, funny, wonderful son Thomas,
With Love from Mom

~ SURPRISE GIFTS ~

Spontaneous, unexpected gifts are the best. Three weeks ago, my husband (who works a 24-hour-a-day shift) called me from work to tell me about a package that had arrived for him the previous day. He knew I wouldn't open the package without his go-ahead, so he told me to go ahead and open it. He said the box contained a variety of music disks. He suggested the disk I should play on my commute to work the following morning. I said sure -- but then, of course, I moved on to some other task without opening the box.

The next morning, in my rush to get out the door and head to work, I nearly forgot about the box. Then I saw it on the table and realized that if I didn't take a minute to open it, my hubby would notice and wonder why. I grabbed a box-cutter, opened the box, removed the suggested disk, headed out the door, and popped the disk into the car's CD player to hear the title tune. Mission accomplished; my work was done. I could tell him later -- without any guilt -- that I did what he asked. (Ha!) But then, as the disk continued to play some familiar and not-so-familiar tunes, something magical happened. Our wedding dance song played on the CD. I hadn't heard it in a while, and (while being somewhat dated by today's standards) it was lovely and sexy, and it set my heart soaring. Time stood still on my commute to work that day.

My husband and I picked a practically perfect dance song to begin our married life: *Set the Night to Music,* by Starship. The funny thing is, it didn't start out that way. We more-or-less settled on it by default. While it was hardly my favorite number or his, we chose this tune because it met our short criteria: it had a sweet melody, and you could dance to it. The clincher, though, was that we both liked it equally. On a scale of one to ten, we agreed it was about a 7.8. Bingo!

This spirit of compromise nicely sums up the formula we've used throughout our married life to keep things harmonious. That my husband can still surprise me (and willingly does) is a very sweet bonus. Here we are, 23-plus years later, still listening to rock 'n roll and still setting the night to music.

~ We Need Another Dr. Seuss ~

Remembering my childhood,
I'll reminisce and pray:
Please, bring another Dr. Seuss
If only for today.

When troubles used to drag us down
Or homework became boring,
His magic words of whimsy always
Sent our spirits soaring:

An elephant named Horton
Was a lovable, sweet nerd.
With stubborn faithfulness and care,
He hatched a baby bird.

As ornery as felines are,
Ted Geisel knew his cats.
Another fave was friendly Bart,
Who wore a lot of hats.

The Sneeches learned humility;
The Grinch embraced the Whos.
The Foot Book offered opposites
While we would tie our shoes.

When reading all these books,
We'd relish every single time
Seuss' brilliant fun with colors
And his genius with a rhyme.

Although some films and animations
Duplicate his glories,
Ted's tales are best told with a book
That illustrates these stories.

This master has no equal.
So, what else is there to say?
We need another Dr. Seuss
If only for today.

October

~ *The Brass Ring* ~

The green reminders are there
Obnoxious lime-colored highlights of what might
have been:
The schedule of dates on a calendar
Signifying rehearsal, tech and performance calls
That never arrived.

Only 24 hours earlier,
Things were different.
I landed the part – fun; challenging yet in my comfort
zone.
It didn't even feel like work, or effort,
Just joy and total acceptance,
And a knowing acknowledgment that for once,
I was totally in the right place at the right time.

Just 24 hours later, those hopes were dashed
Due to obstacles beyond my control.
What should I do? My sister suggested the advice
I once gave her, which was to simply detach.
I went with the journey, took a leap at the brass ring,
And lost,
But not because I had let it slip away. Not this time.

It wasn't my fault. It was just a fact.

Opportunities like this will come and go in our lives.
The important thing I learned is to be there when
they do,
Be present in the moment, be alive;

Especially, be grateful; and know
That in being able, willing and appreciative
Of these golden opportunities,
You will leave yourself open and ready for the next one.

Trust your heart
And don't compromise yourself or your values in the process,
Because everything is a process.
It's called Life, and it's a glorious, marvelous adventure!

As long as I'm able to climb back on the seat
I plan to enjoy the ride.
You might consider it, too –
The view looks pretty darn great from where I sit.

~ *Just Dessert* ~

Once upon a time
there was a kingdom without sweets
Meals would consist
of bread, milk, vegetables and meats.

But then one day, the country's queen
said meals were a bore;
The food she ate was good,
but she desired something more.

What would make it more complete,
and quench her appetite?
A sugar snack to start the meal
might offer new delight.

To please the queen, the royal court
and townsfolk made a bet
To come up with a scrumptious
recipe for choco'late.

They knew it was her favorite treat,
and it would be ideal
To have a brownie, cake or pie
to serve before each meal.

One handsome lad was awfully smart,
and something of a flirt
He said, "Let's make that serving *last*.
They call it a 'dessert.'"

The testy king said, "Wait a sec,"
as he and his queen dined.
"You can't throw out a word unless
that word can be defined."

The young man didn't miss a beat:
"The word is from the French.
It means 'to serve' and then, 'to clear
the table or the bench.'"

"Dessert is like … a glass of wine
once you have had your fish.
It is a tasty, sweet reward
that follows your last dish."

"Think candy, cherry cheesecake,
pudding, chocolate cookie bites;
"Plus popsicles and apple pie
with ice cream --- all delights..."

(The royal court's mouths watered
as they turned to face the throne.
The king looked toward his wife,
who was to make this choice alone.)

"…this is why dessert should be
the *last* course of the meal.
Would you eat a chocolate torte
and follow it with veal?"

The people laughed at that,
but no one louder than the queen!
And by decree, this final course
became a glad routine.

The lad soon fell in love
with this queen's daughter -- no mistake!
And launched a *new* tradition
at their wedding, with a cake.

We should never feel guilty
for this tempting interlude,
'Cuz dessert's the "royal" treat we get
for finishing our food.

~ Loss ~

When we're older, we know we will lose people to death because it's inevitable.
What we *don't* expect to lose are friendships – especially old ones.
But sometimes we do.
People move, they change, they move on, and relationships change too.
Whether it's because of some unplanned event
That has an unexpected and profound effect on the other person,
or whether it's because of a falling-out, or mere boredom with the other person,
it happens. And it happens a lot more frequently than we would like to admit.

Sometimes we don't know about it until many months later,
because they've quietly moved on and we haven't.
This type of loss can be sadder, and much more deeply felt, than someone's death.
The most painful losses are those you feel
when the other person is still walking around, living his or her life,
working, eating, playing, loving, and ultimately thriving
all without you there to share in it, to witness it, or even to talk about it
because they simply don't need or want you there.

The death of a friend or loved one is a grief that is shared by many

and it can even be a gentle, welcome and healing sort of grief

because it gives us full permission to reminisce with others about the happy, sad and heartfelt moments

that we shared with the loved one when he or she was alive.

We mourn the death by celebrating the loved one's life with formal services,

warm receptions, food, drink, their favorite music, their beloved photos.

And while we mourn, there is sympathy – even if we never recover from the loss.

The loss of a friendship, on the other hand,

is a grief that is felt by only one. We are alone in our suffering.

It is a cruel grief caused not only by the loss itself -- the person we miss --

but also by the inevitable sense of betrayal and rejection.

Such a loss can redefine our lives and make us question everything.

When the loss is still expressed months later, it is met not so much with sympathy

as with anguished demands that we get over it already.

There is no party to mark the occasion; no gravesite to mark the passing.

When a friendship dies, a little bit of hope dies with it.

~ *Midnight* ~

He was beautiful and well-bred
He had a long gorgeous shiny jet-black mane
And soulful dark-chocolate eyes
His body was muscular, firm and shapely
He was my best friend and he loved me
We were like Heathcliff and Catherine – well, sort of
We would go riding in the hills together at dusk
He was a stallion and his name was Midnight.

One day, my father said he'd take me to
the carnival that was coming to town
I wanted to go, of course, but only
if Midnight would ride me
My dad didn't mind; after all, he was the one
from whom I learned to appreciate horses
The next thing I knew, we were there
The carnival was lined with booths that had
handmade crafts, goodies to eat,
And various prize-winning games
Like Lucky Toss and Balloon Darts and Duck Convoys.
There were cotton candy, peanuts, popcorn, ice
cream cones, hot dogs and cold drinks...
But my absolutely favorite thing about
the carnival was always the rides:
The Ferris wheel, the Tilt-A-Whirl,
the makeshift Roller Coaster,
And especially the Merry-Go-Round.
I was fascinated just watching the carousel
horses. They were joyous and romantic.

There was a dentist's chair in the middle of the carnival.
My dad was sitting there…getting a shave and a haircut.
Right around the corner I spotted my
favorite ride, the Merry-Go-Round.
It was too late for me to get on
But as I listened to the festive "Da-Da-
Lee-Tee" of the Piano-Bar music
I saw a familiar black horse spinning
by me, again and again…
It was Midnight! I just knew it.
Somehow he had managed to become
mounted to the carousel.
A young lady with beautiful blonde
ringlets was riding my Midnight.
I called out to my beloved horse but he couldn't hear me.
The centrifugal motion made it impossible for
him to break away -- I was afraid for him.
"Midnight! Midnight!" I called out.
But the harder I cried, the faster the
carousel seemed to go.
It was as if Midnight didn't *want* to hear me.
At that moment I feared all was lost.

I turned away from the lights and the
motion and the carnival music
And as I did, the images vanished like
characters erased from a chalkboard.
The dentist's chair was still there but it was now empty
And all was quiet like a ghost town, so I headed home.
I dreamt of my dear, departed dad that night.
When I woke up, there was light
shining through my window.
I checked the clock. It was Midnight.

102

~ *Mister Twister* ~

On an autumn day I saw you
You looked so distant, so mysterious
I will never understand why I stood in line
Just to meet you
I hate lines.
Why do the young at heart
Continually take a ride that they know won't last
In order to be able to say,
"I was there, so let me tell you what it was like."
For, so many of us go through that
We stand in line time and time again
Just to enjoy a few fleeting moments of our lifetimes
Only to say, "I'll never go back again."

But you, my friend,
I often wonder if you've ever been there
Because you threw me for a curve
You twisted my heart
You took me up
And then you let me down again –
Quickly, suddenly
Scarcely giving me a chance
To catch my breath
But when I was finally able to get up and walk away
I knew I was okay – I was alive.

Our relationship reminds me of a roller coaster ride
Where time stood still from start to end
And when it was all over I began to wonder why
And I wished that I could buy another ticket
And take the ride again.

November

~ *Broken Crayon* ~

November 22, 1963
Our president – prominent, beloved, charismatic –
Was now dead.
    Television images of the Plaza played constantly
    Like a record with a broken needle –
    Over and over and over again.
        The hours turned into days
        We saw the funeral
        The strong and solemn widow, the stoic
        daughter
        The proud and patriotic young son
        And the nation wept.
            It felt like house arrest for me
            Silent, dreary and dark – I was but a child
            But November, the month of my birth,
            Was forever altered.

My older sister saw me sitting alone
At the kitchen table
With a box of crayons
And an empty piece of paper.
    I wept silently
    While the television blared
    Touched, she asked me why I cried.
        "My crayon broke," I replied
        As I held the snapped blue-green evidence
        In my hand.
            My favorite color
            Broken in two pieces
            Destroyed forever.

~ *Disappointment* ~

It may come without warning
And at times without words

Sometimes it sneaks up on you
And other times it hits you in the face
Sudden, unexpected, and unwelcome

Or it comes to you in a piece of news –
Nothing devastating; sometimes barely noticeable

But then it eats at you slowly, microscopically,
Like a parasite,
Uninvited, unwanted, and relentless

In its need to grow within you,
To become you,
Until you have no choice but to notice,

To acknowledge, to face it --
And somehow attempt to correct it.

How destructive. How damaging.
How terribly, terribly disappointing.

~ Insomnia ~

Sometimes I lie
Awake at night
And in my mind
I start to write

Epiphanies I don't invite
These sudden flashes of insight
Are met with vague but sheer delight
And sometimes too, a little fright

For after all, it's near midnight
So, struggling with this inner fight,
I grab a pen.
Adjust my sight.

I have no choice!
'though try I might,
I'd lose all recall
At first light.

~ Joseph ~

Being kept waiting isn't the worst thing in the world.
Waiting to be called for jury duty,
I read a book about Joseph*, King of Dreams,
And wearer of the magnificent multicolored coat
Given to him by his adoring father, Jacob.
I had heard about Joseph and the coat as a youngster
And thought at the time that the
coat was the whole story.
It was merely the beginning of a
fascinating and sad tale.

The story of Joseph is about much
more than a beautiful covering.
It is a man's journey from innocence,
arrogance and lofty dreams
To hard lessons learned. Joseph's journey took him
From his brothers' jealousy and betrayal
To torture, slavery, and scandal; and then,
To goodness, strength, intelligence,
resourcefulness and forgiveness.
It is the story of a life of honor.
Learning of Joseph's remarkable adventures
In the course of the two days I reported for jury duty
Forever changed me.

Throughout those two days, I never
was called to sit on a jury.
I was released – and a little disappointed, frankly.
Yet in those short hours I learned
what it means to be patient

And to experience true grace
against overwhelming odds.
Who was I to complain? Who *am* I to
complain? About anything?
Thank you, Joseph.

Genesis 37 – 50.

~ Lesson Plan on Aging ~

You know you're getting older when...

1. There's a zero at the end of your age.
2. Wrinkle lines appear on your face overnight. Worse, your hands look like Google maps in 3-D.
3. You can proudly name songs from the 60s, 70s and 80s, but struggle to name 5 new ones.
4. You remember how good-looking Paul Newman was before the spaghetti sauce and salad dressing.
5. Your favorite shoes are a pair of slippers.
6. You run to the store wearing patterned sweats (PJs).
7. The highlight of your Saturday is watching an old black-&-white movie classic on TCM.
8. However, a good marathon is never out of the question. (Check out the ones on Me-TV.)
9. One glass of wine puts you to sleep. So does one cup of coffee.
10. Articles and advice on diet, exercise, and lifestyle improvements cause irritable bowel syndrome.
11. Those annoying drivers who maintain too-safe distances and never exceed the limit? I'm a happy member of that club.
12. Your directional dysfunctionality goes into overdrive. Literally.
13. "Late at night" used to be after midnight; it's now 9 pm.
14. You over-explain, which means you give the term, then the definition. To clarify, this is called over-explaining.

15. You become invisible.
16. And realize that this may be a good thing.
17. You recognize yourself on this list.
18. You know that this is okay.
19. You wish you could add to it.
20. Here's your chance:

_____

~ *Spiro's Greetings* ~

Outside the tavern stands a sign
Inviting one to drink and dine
Inside, you'll find an air of mirth
Including folks not of this earth.

   It's all insane frivolity
   With darts, pool, video, t.v.
   No stranger than your average bar
   Most everyone knows who you are.

The bartenders are quite alert
Especially one whose name is Kurt
He shares in all festivities
Attentive, fun and aimed to please.

   Spiro's serves the finest ale
   Yes, even when the Seahawks fail
   And when the football game is done
   Some money prizes can be won.

Though recent visits have been rare
I've never not enjoyed it there
Throughout the rain and heavy snows
You'll find a haven at Spiro's.

   A happy holiday to all
   And thanks a lot – I've had a ball!

December

~ *Christmas* ~

The music box with carousel
The village with its dolls
The centerpiece a stable with
Some sheep placed on some straws

The fire's glow adorns the room
Lights twinkle on the tree
Wrapped packages soon multiply
Amid an air of glee ~~

This peaceful scene can only mean
That Christmastime is here,
Yet visions of approaching mirth
Seem more like yesteryear.

Who could have dreamt such thoughtful care
And lavishness would last
When contemplating grimly
On the recent, troubled past?

There is one person I recall
(You, too, are prob'ly able):
A homeless youth, brought forth among
The sheep, the straw and stable.

~ A CHRISTMAS TREASURE ~

The Christmas season always brings to mind happy childhood memories of freshly-cut evergreen trees adorned with bright, cheerful ornaments, glittering tinsel and sparkling lights. My mom would heat spiced apple cider on the stove and we would enjoy home-baked Christmas cookies. Christmas wasn't Christmas without my mom's beloved Nativity set and a musical church that sweetly played *Silent Night*.

My mom made everything beautiful. Yet every year, come Christmas Eve, she would sink into a deep depression. Why, on that day of all days, was she always so sad?

Like lots of kids, I dreamt of a white Christmas. I found it odd that, even though we lived in an area that received plenty of snowfall, it never snowed on Christmas Eve. I mentioned this to my mom, who grew very quiet at first. Then she told me of a particularly snowy Christmas in Chicago where her sister's family lived. As she spoke, I enviously pictured them on Christmas Eve as they watched the wild snow flurries outside, all the while remaining safely inside where it was cozy and warm. My mom said that on one particular Christmas Eve, my aunt was kicking herself because she had gone to the store and forgotten to pick up my fourteen-year-old cousin's favorite dessert of ice cream. It had become an annual tradition for him.

My mom had always gushed about her charismatic young nephew (my cousin). The thing she most admired about him was his positive, can-do spirit. Despite the wind-chill and bitter frost, he volunteered to pick up the ice cream at a nearby store. My aunt told him to forget about it, but he insisted, and bundled himself up and left the house. He never made it back home. Returning from the store with the ice cream tucked under his arm, he was struck and killed by a vehicle that skidded into his path on the treacherous road. I can only pray it happened so fast that it never registered.

It shocked me to learn what happened on that long-ago Christmas Eve. With the night before Christmas forever altered in her mind and heart, how did my mom manage, year after year, to celebrate with us the wonder and joy of that season?

In an odd way, the fact that she continued to carry on in the face of certain despair was its own kind of miracle. Every year as I assemble the Nativity set for our centerpiece, I say a special little prayer for my departed young cousin. He was a family treasure I never had the pleasure to meet. The other Christmas treasure, of course, was Mom.

~ Our Gift ~

The venue's booked, the date is set,
The caterer's been paid
Photographers are interviewed;
Invites will be handmade
The bride and groom are radiant
With love and joy to spare
They even have the bridal party
Knowing what to wear

Yet as the date approaches,
There's the chance that they might fumble!
The details get scattered;
Memories become a jumble
So what should this bride's parents do
As Christmastime draws near?
How do they find a gift
For this sweet couple they hold dear?

Well, it occurred to both of us
A day-of wedding planner
Might handle the exact details
In a "well-thought-out" manner
So, let us on this Christmas Day
Secure your wedded bliss:
A planner for your nuptials...
Our gift to you is this.

We even have someone in mind
The choice is up to you
Please let us know if you approve
And we'll know what to do.

~ *The Tree* ~

Christmas
used to be my
favorite time of year
especially the tree
until the year we got a bushy one
and the cat drank out of the tree stand
and it dried out
and Dad tried to cut it
to make it look healthy
but it ended up crooked in the stand
and we had to leave it and go to Christmas mass.
The Christmas lights twinkling from the window
reminded me of the *Titanic* –
brightly lit, but listing heavily and sinking fast.
I mentioned it to Dad, who wisely
went back inside and unplugged the lights.
The tree "survived" that year, but just barely.
Dad turned it into a tabletop.
It was such a spectacle for the neighbors
that we thought of putting an
Espresso sign in the window
so we could make a buck from the exhibition.
Ever since that disaster, we've saved
time and gotten a tabletop.
*****

Believe it or not,
Christmas is still my favorite time of year
just *not* especially the tree.

~ *Two Visitors* ~

This year I have two Christmas trees --
One is artificial, tiny, with nothing but a circle of lights
And one real, very tall, handsomely decorated, skinny,
With only a few lights that flash off and on.
Only a half-dozen work, and not very well.

I have a bag of gifts from my sister
Which I place under the tall, skinny tree.
My brother stops by and we go to breakfast.
I order a tuna sandwich on toast and a Coke.
He orders a burger and coffee.
Afterwards, I invite my brother over
And we light the Christmas tree lights.

There is a good movie on television – it's an "oldie."
As we sit back to watch it,
There's a knock on the door.
It's my sister. She's stopping by with more gifts.
I invite her to stay,
But she has to go.

As she turns to leave, she remarks how strange it is
That I have two trees, and she laughs.
My brother doesn't think it's strange.
In many ways, we're twins.
I'll place my sister's new gifts under the tiny artificial tree.
It will complete the ensemble nicely, I think.

~ IT'S A WONDERFUL MOVIE ~

Not all movie experiences occur inside of a darkened theater, but rather, in the comfort of our homes surrounded by loved ones. My mom spoke fondly of a movie that was released shortly after the end of World War II. It had been years since she had seen it, and she said it was a small film and not very well-received. It fizzled at the box office and disappeared quickly.

Still, she had had the distinct pleasure of catching it during its short run, and said it was easily one of her favorite movies of all time. The movie was *It's a Wonderful Life*, a sad, simple tale of a small-town businessman who battles as much against his own demons as he does against the town Scrooge, Mr. Potter, to keep corruption out of Bedford Falls. This was before the movie had become part of the public domain. One night it was on network television and it had already started, but we sat down to watch it anyway. I don't recall the scene I came into on that first viewing, but I was curiously captivated. Although I knew that sort of David-vs.-Goliath sentimentality didn't work in real life, the film and its star had such an idealistic charm that I was hooked on Jimmy Stewart after that.

Several years later, my mom and I attended the opening production of the stage play *Harvey* at a Denver playhouse. There was a surprise announcement that Jimmy Stewart and his wife Gloria were in the audience. We didn't have tickets to the reception following the show, but we were stuck in the theater waiting for a cab that never arrived. An hour later, we found ourselves alone in the lobby with the Stewarts for several heart-stopping moments. We exchanged pleasantries (I squeaked out a "hello") and briefly discussed the chilly Colorado weather. A short time later the Stewarts were joined by *Harvey*'s author, Mary Chase, and her handsome male secretary, who kindly offered us a ride home.

Like the story of Bedford Falls, those things don't happen in real life – but it really did. Another thing I've learned is that the best movie experiences breed rich experiences of their own. And the ones that are shared with those we love are the most treasured experiences of all.

~ THANK YOU ~

If events happened in our lives
As quickly as they happen in our dreams
Or in our thoughts
Then we'd all be insane –

This is why I write.
It enables me to study my thoughts and dreams
And think about what they mean.

I'd be writing songs too,
If I could record music on paper
Because I hear music in my dreams
Beautiful songs I've never heard...

But I don't write music
And can never remember the songs
The next day when I'm able to record them.

We all have the capacity for creativity
If we'd only listen to our dreams
And act on them once in a while.

Thank you for "listening" to mine.

My Educational Tour

My Educational Tour

Notes from a tour in Europe that
was sponsored by Kennedy
Catholic High School (formerly John F.
Kennedy Memorial High School),
taken with my daughter Emily in the summer of '09.

Teresa Mosteller

6/18-19 -- SEA → Newark → London, U.K.

It was my original intention to write something every day, but I'm three days into my European vacation already and this is my first entry. The trip started relatively uneventfully. Gordy took us to breakfast at Denny's, and then drove us to the airport. The wait at the airport was interminable. We were supposed to board at around 11:58 a.m. but didn't leave the ground until around 3:45 p.m.

There was a thunderstorm in Newark, NJ, our first destination. Then they put us on a plane that needed to be "taped" – whatever that means – but it sounded ominous. Turbulence on the flight was heavy, but otherwise the first leg of the flight was uneventful.

The second leg of our flight, from Newark to London, was, too, except for the preteen who sat next to me talking my ear off until she fell asleep and plopped her head directly into my lap. I was desperate to move her off me, but was afraid her neck might snap if I made the attempt. She was completely out of it. Emily thought it was pretty funny, but I got no sleep on the flight. (As my mom would have said, hardy, har har.)

6/19 -- London, U.K.

We had tickets to a show, and since our flight was so late, we didn't have time to check into our hotel or eat anything beforehand. We left our luggage on the commuter bus. The good news: the show was *Wicked.* It was at the Victoria Palace Theatre (Westminster borough). What I saw of it was great! But I was so exhausted from the travel, the long waits between flights, and the fact that I didn't sleep on either plane, that I dozed through a small portion of Act I. I woke up and, feeling quite self-conscious, shot a quick glance toward Emily, who I was sure would be ashamed and embarrassed for me. She was out like a light. I detected a tiny little snore coming from her general direction. It might have even been one of the students sitting on her opposite side. We were all extremely tired.

Afterwards, I steered Emily and me to the wrong exit and we were late meeting up with the group for the return to our hotel. She didn't speak to me for the rest of the night, which was okay because I was so out of it by then that I couldn't have held up my end of the argument anyway. To give credit where it was due, she'd handled things pretty well up to that point, and this is all a brand-new experience for her. Still, I felt depressed and sad, not to mention broke and a little frantic about my money situation. (I found out that the exchange office didn't take credit, and I had only a few British pounds on me.)

6/20 -- London, U.K.

Our time in London consisted of the usual touristy things, but it was a lovely day both weather-wise and in my attitude, which needed an infusion of goodwill. My legs are cramping but I'm getting around okay. We saw Buckingham Palace and the Changing of the Guard, which was like a big parade with an impeccably dressed marching band. After that we went to Leicester Square where Emily, several of her friends, and I bought ice cream. Then, we joined up with the full group and had dinner at an Indian restaurant. We also went on a city tour and saw Big Ben, the Tower Bridge, Parliament, Westminster Abbey, the London Eye Ferris wheel, the Tower of London, and a few other places.

Lest anyone be envious about this tour -- well, we viewed it all from our bus seats. The one stop we made on the entire tour was to a gift shop. I fell for it – I purchased a t-shirt and a deck of Union Jack cards for Thomas (he collects playing cards). I'm also picking up rocks at each site we visit to bring home to Thomas. He likes rocks.

6/21 -- U.K. → Paris, France

We took the Channel Tunnel (Chunnel), the high-speed train, from London to Paris. After we arrived, we went on a walking tour of Versailles. Very, very tiring. When will my feet get a break?! Several of us volunteered to take a second bus to Versailles, and it was a little weird. We had questions for the French people, but I don't speak French very well. We stopped for lunch and had crepes. Not filling, but tasty.

Also, I made sure to grab one or two stones at stops throughout the day.

The group reunited for dinner at L'Escarmouche. We had a delicious beef stroganoff, and chocolate pudding for dessert. Then we went to Notre Dame, which was pretty magnificent. I'm guessing it was the inspiration for the large stained-glass window at the West Seattle church where Gordy and I were married. Wishful thinking, maybe -- but that's my story and I'm sticking to it.

We took the Metro (subway) back to our new hotel, the Mercure. It is beautiful – new and clean. But no swimming pool, which is a disappointment to everybody, including me. Dorinda (a parent of one of the other student travelers) was supposed to meet her husband Bob at the hotel, but since our hotel was switched at the last minute, they didn't connect. But there was light at the end of the tunnel: my roommate on the trip, another parent named Kathie, treated me to a delicious iced-cold beer in the lounge. We were joined by Dorinda and Denise (another parent I know). Nice, nice women.

This trip is going to be fun; I feel better about it already.

6/22 -- Paris, France → Einsiedeln, Switzerland

Paris is *magnifique*! I've enjoyed every moment in this special city. Love the language, and *oui*, it does come back to me. One word at a time. Everything I know about Paris I learned from the children's book *Madeline*. We took a city tour by bus and saw the Arch de Triomphe, which is the archway in the boulevard scenes of *Madeline*. We also passed by the Champs Elysees, of course, the name of the long boulevard in *Madeline*. We glimpsed the River Seine, which...well, okay, I was more reminded of the movie *Charade* than of *Madeline* at that point. As it was daylight, I could see that the river was polluted. Still, I would have loved to have taken one of those boat rides that Audrey Hepburn and Cary Grant took in *Charade*. It was so romantic! We also saw the Grand Opera House that was the creative inspiration behind *The Phantom of the Opera*. Then, we took a field trip to the Louvre Museum. The glass pyramid was unexpected but mesmerizing. It didn't quite fit, but it didn't exactly clash, either. It was a bit of a conundrum.

Kathie described the Louvre thusly: the architectural marvel (and marble) of the vaunted walls and ceilings overwhelmed the fine artwork. Very true. It was almost annoying how I had to crane my neck to stare at the most amazing ceilings I'd ever seen. The artwork that adorned the walls was splendid, too. But the Mona Lisa? Overrated. She was mounted in the middle of an otherwise empty wall and was protected from prying hands behind a roped partition. Her portrait is small. The wall almost swallowed her up whole. But I liked actually seeing her -- she was kind of winking, and I felt like I got the joke.

I also enjoyed the Winged Victory (la femme) and the Wedding Party. My favorite piece was the sculpture of the Venus de Milo – more on her later. These pieces don't begin to scratch the surface of the barely-scratched surface I actually saw. I loved it all, and I don't consider myself much of a museum person. It was peaceful and centering there.

I also mastered the Metro today – piece of cake. Earlier worries about my incompetence getting on and off were greatly exaggerated (by me). I could do this every day going to and from work, and enjoy it quite well.

We saw a perfume demonstration, then had dinner at a pizza place before heading over to the Eiffel Tower for a ride to the top. It was as awesome as one could hope to expect. Paris is a marvel to behold from a 360-degree perspective! When we departed, the tower was lit up and looked lovely and fragile. But it's not.

Like the Venus de Milo, my favorite work of art in the Louvre, the Eiffel Tower's strength is in its supposed weakness. Venus, the goddess of love, is flawed and damaged. But it's the flaw that makes you care about her. (I'm writing this on a bus to Switzerland and it's jittery.) We don't know what Venus was holding or trying to protect that was savagely disarmed from her, but she is still standing. (Some say it was an apple; others believe it was a baby.) Likewise, the Eiffel Tower at a distance is all loose-looking limbs, but precious all the same. Up close, it is strong and majestic – so much more impressive than my wildest expectations from *Madeline!* That endearing classic gave me a sweet, yet modest taste of the grandeur of Paris.

As we boarded the Metro from the Eiffel Tower, the Tower's lights were twinkling like a thousand stars. An illuminating end to a glorious day.

Kathie and I had a couple beers at the hotel bar before packing and turning in, in anticipation of another day of travel (next stop, Switzerland). I will miss Paris. French is in my blood, and I felt at home during our short visit.

6/23 -- Einsiedeln, Switzerland

We visited the gorgeous, ornamental monastery/church and school at Einsiedeln (pronounced "high ceiling"). It's also a mausoleum that contains ornate, colorful tombs surrounded by gold and silver inlay. The monastery is resplendent. I can hardly stand it, it's so unreal. It very nearly took my breath away.

We stayed at the St. Georg, and for dinner we had spaghetti, salad, and a block of vanilla ice cream with raspberry sherbet (for dessert). The table where I sat was all male students. Don't ask me how I ended up here; I have no idea. Surprisingly, I wasn't invisible. [One of the students at the table, Nick, is a good friend of Emily's even now.]

Accommodations at the St. Georg were lovely. Kathie and I got a renovated room – one of the few that was renovated – and it was conveniently situated on the first floor of residences. The floors were hardwood; there were several windows that let in lots of natural light; the bathroom was small but clean and pretty. The bed was very comfortable, and I slept well.

There was some drama tonight when one of the students misplaced her passport and holder. To be continued....

6/24 -- Mt. Pilatus and Lucerne, Switzerland

Mt. Pilatus has by far been the "funnest" (not a real word, but still) and most adventurous excursion yet. We rode to nearly the summit by ski lifts (two of them – we transferred to a larger lift near the top) and then walked by stairs the rest of the way to the summit, on a staircase that was built into the rock in a spiral fashion. Then we climbed even more stairs but had to go down a steep, slick, wet flight of stairs to explore some shallow caves. It was tiring, but great exercise; and a great opportunity to grab a couple of stones for my burgeoning collection.

Next, Emily – who's been in a good mood today – asked me what I thought of a snow globe she wanted to purchase for Gordy. She said it was just right and that it was 15 franks. She made a mistake – it was actually 30 franks, so I loaned her some money for the balance. The 15-frank globe was one of those miniatures that don't really count.

So, let me tell you about this snow globe. Inside the globe itself are two cows (actually, a cow and a calf) standing in a green field against a blue sky background. Both cows are adorned with red Swiss-flag-bedecked cowbells around their necks, and they both fashion red bows on the tops of their heads. The cows themselves are milk cows; white with black spots. The base of the snow globe is resin. It is multicolored and depicts a picturesque Swiss landscape and village with quaint structures, road travelers, homesteaders and friendly furry beasts (including several more cows). The snow globe is darling, if a bit cartoonish. The cows are smiling and drooling at the same time. They have a hopeful, hungry look.

I don't know, the overall effect doesn't shout "Dad" to me. It's a personal joke between Emily and him, I guess. She had her heart set on a snow globe for Dad, and this may be her one opportunity to get one, who knows? Even if it is a couple of cows. And why are they standing on a green, grassy field under a clear, blue sky with snow flurries showering down around them? Something isn't right there. And why are we once again stopping at a gift shop? I'm not falling for it. Incidentally, I scored some yummy Swiss candies and will give them to Mom and Grandma Mosteller when we get back home. I also bought some cool Swiss pens and postcards.

The best part of the day was the spectacular 90-minute ferry-boat ride around Lake Lucerne. I enjoyed a delicious cup of coffee (with a delicate side of cream) served in a porcelain cup. The coffee and cream were presented on a porcelain saucer, and they were accompanied by a scrumptious piece of Swiss chocolate. Very civilized! Emily remarked how the ferry boat was *much* nicer than the ones in Seattle. I agree. The ferry boats in Seattle only carry paper cups.

After the lovely and enchanting boat ride, during which I thought I'd died and gone to heaven, we stopped at more gift shops in Lucerne where I picked up additional souvenirs. I also had a light lunch – a sandwich consisting of salami and cheese on a baguette – and coffee with cream at Julius. I purchased a few more postcards and even had a chance to buy some stamps at the post office, to go with all the postcards I now have. They were about two franks apiece (nearly 30 franks total) – expensive! But, at least I had them.

Dinner was chicken noodle soup, veal, French fries, mixed veggies and a delicious Neapolitan ice cream (chocolate, vanilla, and mocha with chocolate chips) for dessert. (I'd had no idea until now that "Neapolitan" is named for Naples, Italy, where the ice cream apparently originated. I feel really smart right now...or really stupid, depending on the moment's perspective.)

Kathie and I have started a nightly ritual – a very enjoyable one — of going to the hotel bar for a beer before bedtime every night. We started doing this in France. We had beers with Dorinda, Denise, Sue and Terry (Sue's husband). John and Melanie, the other chaperones, joined us for beers the first night we were in Switzerland. Jeff (another chaperone) and Angela (Kennedy History instructor) stopped by, too. We also have Steve and Carol with us; they're lovely people.

Naturally, the day isn't complete without a little drama, and today there were two. There was 1) the situation with the lost passport and pouch, which was drawn out to almost cruel proportions, because one of the chaperones didn't think the girl who misplaced them was "upset" enough to earn them back. Fortunately, they were found. And, 2) another student who happens to be a vegetarian didn't know she had to preorder her vegetarian meal and went without dinner tonight. Her request for a vegetarian meal apparently angered one of our drivers and one of the chaperones. All I can say is, I'm glad I'm not a student on this trip.

I will miss Switzerland. By far, it has been my favorite country on our trip up until now. My favorite city, however, is undeniably Paris.

6/25 -- Lucerne, Switzerland → Florence, Italy

Day eight already. *Bon journo*! People were prancing around, saying "Bidet! Bidet!" (pronounced "bee-day") I thought it was Italian for "Good day!" Suffice it to say, it's a great invention.

We drove on a bus from Switzerland to a lovely Tuscan district of Italy outside of Florence. The bus ride was a pleasant one. I sat by myself, but behind Kirk and Max, who kept asking me if I was comfortable because their seats were in the partial recline positions and they were encroaching on my legroom. Later I overheard Max talking to Denise about the Seattle Opera. He sang and even soloed for the opera when he was young, and was in *La Boehme*. Then, when his voice started to change, he was a supernumerary (non-singing ensemble player) for the opera. I asked him if he knew my friend Paula, who works there, and he said yes – he really liked working with her. He asked me to say hi the next time I saw her.

We all had a nice but pricey lunch on the road – a roadside cafeteria/mart, basically. Emily had tortellini and ravioli and I had salad, focaccia and a shrimp & rice dish.

We arrived in Tuscany around 5:00 pm. Kathie and I had a lovely room with the only balcony on our side of the building -- amazing! We felt very blessed. We got a chance to enjoy delicious coffees on the balcony, and we hung our laundry to dry on the "line," courtesy of Kathie. Very clever.

Dinner was pasta (a mainstay in Italy), a chicken dish and eggplant. It was very good. It was followed by a refreshing salad, and watermelon for dessert. We hurried through dinner so we could take a bus ride to Pisa and see the famous Leaning Tower. It was a sight to behold. Circa 1100. It's in the process of another renovation. The certainty that it would eventually topple is no longer a certainty at all.

So, here's a brief history lesson on the Leaning Tower of Pisa. (Feel free to skip this paragraph if you know the history already.) It's a tourist attraction due to its fascinating history. It was built as a bell-tower for the Cathedral/ Duomo – Romanesque Pisan Church in Pisa, a lovely but sadly poverty-stricken place with lots of street vendors plying their fake wares. The erection of the bell-tower was suspended on several occasions, then resumed, then suspended again. It took years before it was completed and the lean became prominent – and uncorrectable – when they were working on the third floor of the tower. The builders thought it would right itself by the time they started work on the fifth floor, thinking that with the design they'd be able to balance it to a straight position, but of course that never happened and the rest is architectural history. The tower continued to lean conspicuously to the right. I didn't count them, but I think the tower has eight floors total. The lean has become a *fait accompli* after all these years. It's the lean that makes the tower a famous landmark.

We returned late – between 11:00-11:30 pm – but still enjoyed our customary wines and beers -- Kathie, Dorinda, Terry, Sue, and me. The drama of the day/evening came late, with a chaperone disciplining one of the boy students for kissing one of the girl students. It sounded innocent to me, but apparently such behavior violates the contract that the kids signed. As scandals go, I guess it will have to do.

6/26 -- Florence, Italy

We traveled there by bus, again. (If you don't like to travel by bus, let's face it -- you probably won't like Europe.) Florence is an interesting city – bigger and grittier than I expected, with some districts that look poor and a bit rundown. Tourist spots everywhere! – but I did find some good buys at the Leather Shop, where we watched a cool leather-making demonstration. The young man who presented the demonstration was cute, and a good salesman. But he was surprisingly brusque as I was walking through a corridor after making my purchases. Apparently, his warm, personable façade only extended to the demonstration counter and the cashier's booth.

I was in a buying mood, and purchased a pair of earrings for 25€ for a friend back home. I also bought a beautiful black leather passport holder and got it engraved with my initials for free. There was a line so it did keep the group -- not waiting, because they all went their separate ways -- but leaving without me. Dorinda, bless her heart, came back for me. I joined her group, which is actually Jeff's group. All young men except for Dorinda and Denise, who both are parents of two of the male students.

Here's where our European adventure took a major turn for the worse – or the better, depending on your perspective.

First, we had lunch at a very nice outdoor café. I had a bruschetta and beer. The guys had pizzas. Dorinda had what I had, and Denise had what looked like a delicious calzone. I put the whole thing on my credit card, and they paid me back with euros.

Sometime after lunch, we took a tour of the Museum of Science (4.50€). It turned out to be a rip-off because two of its three floors were closed for renovation. Mostly about Galileo; partly Leonardo de Vinci, many telescopes and visual artifacts of discoveries that they made about earth and space and time. Galileo's finger, which had been cruelly cut off, was supposed to have been preserved in a jar in the museum, but I never saw it. The museum's curator, who sold us the tickets, failed to tell us that two-thirds of the museum was off-limits for renovation for the grand reopening in September 2009.

After leaving the Museum of Science, we all stopped and enjoyed delicious gelato cones. We also took a short guided walking tour to a church and around the square. I must say, I tremendously enjoyed the magnificent scenery outside of the square – a fine statue of David. I was hardly the only one who liked it.

With time to kill before we needed to return for dinner, we voted on what to do next and decided to hike up to a fort – the Forte di Belvedere. (I'm on a jittery bus again on our drive to Assisi as I'm writing this.) The path to the fort was a winding, uphill walk and even steep in parts. It had been raining intermittently throughout the day – sometimes showering – but still, we managed to make our way to the top of the winding fort. I was the last one to arrive. I was tired, and anxious for a rest.

It wasn't to be. The fort was closed on account of the sudden and recent, tragic death of a young woman perhaps a day or two earlier. Her name was Veronica Lakotelli and she was a pretty blonde woman; possibly a student of the university. Her picture was displayed prominently on the entrance to the fort, and on various portions of the surrounding grounds of the fort.

So next, Dorinda suggested we try the botanical gardens, which were a short walk from the fort. No dice. The botanical gardens were closed, cut off; no explanation given.

We decided to head back down (downhill, thank God, or so we thought) and do some shopping or whatever before heading back to the Palazzo Vecchio / square – I think that's the name of the place, anyway, where our groups were supposed to reunite at 5:45 for supper. It was around 3:00 pm and I was just telling Max that this was one of my favorite times of the day. I felt glad it had stopped raining.

That's when it happened. Seemingly out of nowhere (but obviously from the heavens), we had a sudden deluge of torrential rain accompanied by lightning and thunder. We were stopped in our tracks. I was wearing a sundress (not a good thing) and flip-flops (a good thing, but they were slippery). A literal river of mud flowed freely down the steep hill where we'd been walking. We stood there for maybe twenty minutes, getting soaked but staying somewhat sheltered underneath an open awning against the rear of a large old, brick building.

Denise, Dorinda and I huddled together to keep warm, which wasn't possible because of the pouring rain. Fortunately, Dorinda had intuitively bought an umbrella earlier that same day. She opened it and allowed the three of us to hover underneath it for partial shelter. It wasn't wide enough to protect all three of us from the elements. It only covered a portion of my head, but it was better than nothing.

Finally, after twenty or so minutes with no end of rain in sight, the boys' chaperone Jeff kindly handed plastic ponchos to Denise and me and said, "let's walk." The ponchos were lifesavers, but we weren't kidding ourselves, it was still miserable. My feet hurt, especially the pinch-y points between my toes; it was slick and slippery; very, very wet, downhill and scary. The poncho kept most of the dampness off me, anyway!

We all managed to ford the river we had to cross – a river of mud – to get to the other side of the street. I think an hour went by like this – walking, slipping, sliding, and occasionally stopping for shelter in the downpour.

Next stop: Cappuccino! We came across a very nice coffee, pastry and chocolate shop. It was a truly welcome site after the unexpected thunderstorm we braved. The first thing I did when I arrived at the café was to make a mash dash to the restroom for a pit stop. (Isn't it funny how water makes you have to go?) The wait staff was kind and accommodating, and things immediately took a turn for the better. The refreshments could not have been more to my liking. The coffee was hot and flavorful, and the chocolate pastry I ordered was pure heaven.

And the rain finally stopped!

Even after all that, we made it back to the square one hour early. Max wanted to shop for an egg, I think for his grandmother, the decorative Faberge type. I asked Dorinda to join us because she has good instincts about those things. But it was a touristy mall square; we didn't find anything. Earlier, we had visited a musical instrument store. Sam's a musician and he wanted to check out a guitar. He said the shopkeeper was a "jerk." It was unlike him to talk like that, so I figured it must be true.

The shopkeeper seemed to be suspicious of the students in our group. Sam said the shopkeeper became enraged when he saw the kids looking at guitars; the shopkeeper became angry again when he saw Sam standing against a life-sized speaker. Sam is very respectful of musical equipment, but the clerk must have thought the students were going to steal something...like a life-sized speaker. I guess I can't blame him. It was clear that our group was just there to look, and not actually make any purchases.

Following that adventure, the guys and I walked toward the square where we spied one of my favorite things – a carousel. While a handful of us jumped on for an old-fashioned carousel ride, Dorinda captured a few pictures of us laughing and enjoying ourselves. Lord knows, we needed that diversion after the wild day we'd had. It's those little, spontaneous moments that have been the most fun, and the most meaningful to me on this vacation.

We returned to the square after that. Emily had arrived, and I regaled her (and the others in my group regaled the others in their respective circles) with wild tales of our grand adventure in the storming, scary rain. Emily had bought two adorable gifts for cousin Jack – a stuffed Mickey Mouse with "Firenza" (Florence) on it, and a darling Pooh bear. She bought both items in the Disney store in the square, where she said she spent an entire hour while the rainstorm was pummeling our group. After she showed me her purchases, I bragged that I'd scored a couple of stones earlier in the day. They were damp, but not worse for the wear.

At 5:45 we all went to dinner -- pasta with a meat-and-tomato-sauce dish. The meat was very good. It tasted like turkey, but I wasn't sure if it was turkey or chicken. We also had potatoes (lots of carbs), apple slices, water, and bread with olive oil and vinaigrette.

We boarded the bus and went back to our Tuscan village. I returned to my room to pack for the next day's trip to Assisi. We're leaving Florence for Rome. Emily came up to my room and we had a nice visit. Then she, Kathie and I joined Terry, Sue, Denise, Dorinda, and Jeff for refreshments.

Later still, at the suggestion of the dark-haired chaperone (from Daniel's group), we took a lovely stroll to where there was a men's a cappella concert in the Cathedral square not far from our hotel. It made a great backdrop. The singers had wonderful voices. Most of the songs were solemn, if lovely, but they also sang "King of the Road" and the crowd really enjoyed that one. We clapped along, but didn't sing along, because it was sung in Finnish.

The only thing that marred the loveliness of it all was a vague but permeating pee aroma in the outdoor square. It was quite unsavory. It made us laugh, though – such a puzzle. Later that evening, Kathie, Dorinda, and I, on our second or maybe third wind by this point, had another nightcap before calling it a night. I live for these nightcaps!

Of course, the evening didn't end without more drama, probably the best yet. But I don't want to talk about it now – I'll talk about it later.

There is actually one big thing I forgot to mention, that I learned about at breakfast this morning. Michael Jackson died of cardiac arrest last night. The medics tried to revive him for an hour, but he was lost. Farrah Fawcett (who had been fighting cancer for some time) also died, either last night or early this morning.

Throughout the day I found myself glancing at all the newsstands and kiosks for articles and photos about Michael Jackson. However, since all the papers were written in Italian, all I could make out was "Michael Jackson" and his photo splashed across the front pages. I found myself wishing, however briefly, that I were back in the States so I could learn more about this tragic event, and also about Farrah Fawcett. It was rather unsettling to be on the other side of the world, with news like this back home.

I wanted to write that it was a peaceful end to an enchanting, if periodically intense, day. But I couldn't sleep for thinking about the loss of these two amazingly talented people. I realize a lot of people thought Michael was some kind of loony-tunes, and maybe even a child molester, but I didn't buy into those stories. Well, maybe the loony-tunes stories, a little. And yet, I admired his talent immensely. That never changed. I felt regret for Farrah Fawcett's death, too -- particularly that her sad demise was overshadowed by the shocking and sensational news of Michael Jackson.

6/27 -- Florence → Assisi → Rome, Italy

Our bus travels today took us from Florence to Rome. I'm writing this on the evening of the 28th and I'm very tired, so I may forget a few details. Everyone here has been terrific, and I appreciate them more than words can say – Dorinda, Denise, Kathie, Jeff, the group leaders Terry, Sue, Angela, John, Carol, Steve; tour guide Pauline; even the other tour guide Daniel, who is a bit full of himself. And Carol and Jovinda and Mel.

It was an 8-9-hour drive with a stopover for lunch. I don't recall what I ate, or where. We drove from Florence through the town of Perugia, to Assisi. Perugia is a university town located halfway between Florence and Rome, and the campus is breathtakingly lovely. Perugia has been featured in the news at home lately, because a West Seattle resident came here as an exchange student and ended up serving a prison term for an unsolved murder. [She was later acquitted.]

After driving on the highway outside of Perugia and passing field after field of beautiful, rich-looking sunflowers, we drove to Assisi. I really enjoyed Assisi. I also enjoyed the fields and fields of sunflowers. They were amazing! And it was a great feeling to be in Assisi, a place I never in my wildest dreams thought I would ever see. St Francis is from Assisi, and he's one of my favorite saints. Assisi is a quiet, peaceful, very quaint town – really lovely.

I had a quick sandwich and coffee there, bought some souvenirs (mainly rosaries) and of course saw the church where St. Francis himself is buried. But once there, I forgot to look at his tomb. I traveled all this way and then missed the biggest attraction. Naturally, I didn't overlook the several fine gift shops in Assisi -- where I made several more, small but meaningful purchases. I don't even like to shop back home, but I find myself doing quite a lot of it over here.

We boarded the bus for Rome, and in the evening, had dinner in the dining room of our latest hotel. Unfortunately, it wasn't very good – the pasta was okay, but the meat tasted like spam, the three-four French fries I had were soggy, and there were no veggies. Dessert was a dry chocolate and vanilla cake.

Following our supper, we piled into the bus and went on a drive to see Rome at night. We saw the outside of Circus Maximus, the Pantheon, Trevi Fountain, and the Colosseum and St. Peter's Basilica; and enjoyed gelato in the Trevi Fountain square.

Today is my seventeenth wedding anniversary, and Kathie let me borrow her phone to call home. Gordy and Thomas were there. We had a good, but brief, chat and Emily said hi to Dad as well. Thomas misses me. He was excited about all the fish he caught on his fishing trip with Dad – he caught 13 to Gordy's 12. I told him I had picked up a few things for him: cards, rocks and a t-shirt (I didn't tell him what the items were). I probably need to get more. The day ended after beers with Kathie and Dorinda. A good end to a satisfying (if relatively uneventful) day. And no drama!

6/28 -- Rome, Italy

Roma! Vatican City and the Colosseum. We went through the Sistine Chapel and saw the gravesites of the popes, including Popes John Paul II, John XXIII, and Paul VI. Then we left the building of the Vatican and stood outside in the courtyard of the magnificent St. Peter's Basilica, where Pope Benedict gave his blessing. I only saw his arm from the open-air balcony window. He could have been anybody, but his arm sure looked like a pope's arm. For the blessing I brought my new rosaries and the two statues of St. Francis of Assisi that I'd bought in Assisi; as well as my Celtic cross necklace (brought from home), and Emily had her new rosary to be blessed. While in the Basilica, Emily and I both touched the cross that in so doing would absolve you of your sins.

Elsewhere on our Vatican City excursion, we were shown the artistically stunning Sistine Chapel and the tomb of St. Peter. The tomb was the size of a small apartment. It was enclosed in glass, so you could see the inside of it. In my humble estimation, it was inviting enough for someone to actually live there (if it weren't already a tomb).

The best thing about today was actually our *next* excursion, to the Roman Colosseum. It was an awesome and inspiring spectacle. Just being there, I felt like I'd gone back in time. It made me think of *The Gladiator.* I want to see that movie again, just so I can see the un-stubby, unbroken Colosseum in the film. It's funny, because all my life I've read and heard about the ruins of ancient civilizations like Greece and Rome. "Ruins" are meant in the literal sense here. So many things are broken, but they're still here, and they are historic landmarks – not demolished or cleared out to make room for another high-rise building. The Colosseum had once been huge and grand, forbidding in its own way because it was a prison of sorts, but it was partially destroyed by earthquakes. Years and years of wear and tear did the rest. It was the most amazing thing I'd ever seen (to date) with my own two eyes.

While standing in the middle of the arena I reached down and picked up a small stone. (Incidentally, Kathie taught me this trick, and I have to say it's a good one – it's like marking territory, but better.) I'm excited about presenting my humble collection of small rocks and stones to Thomas when I get home. I've collected stones from most of the places we've visited. This is no small thing – these stones are ancient!

A stone from the Colosseum seems especially meaningful. I almost feel guilty about it, like I'm removing a piece of hallowed ground. I shared this feeling with someone else, who said not to worry – a single stone wasn't likely to be missed.

Our group had about 45 minutes for lunch. I looked for Emily, but couldn't find her. She was mad at me for some reason. Dorinda invited me to join a few other adults for lunch. We found a beer & pizza place. I was going to use my credit card and request reimbursement from the others, which would have given me an infusion of cash, but the restaurant didn't take credit so I paid 15€.

After lunch we all headed back to the group for more walking. Coincidentally, Nick and Max were at the same restaurant as us. We found out later that we were supposed to get a ride on the coach to see Trevi Fountain, but we ended up walking there instead. I was thoroughly exhausted. My feet started to blister. We arrived at Trevi Fountain and everyone broke up into groups to get gelato. I was going to, but first decided to put my socks on to protect my sore, blistered feet. I sat on the steps of the large corner church, but right after I did, a friendly priest came out and waved me away so he could close the gate. Feeling somewhat dejected, I limped over to where Emily was seated to put on my socks. Max was sitting across from her and offered me his seat. I took it.

After Trevi Fountain, we walked for what seemed like another hundred blocks or so to the Spanish steps. I didn't want to go up them, but had to go down them because we were all supposed to meet at the bottom of the steps in an hour or so. I looked up the 'up' flight of steps, and they towered over me like a mountain. Fortunately, we had a bit of free time. I ended up walking alone for the most part, after chatting with Carol and Mel a bit, and didn't know what to do with myself after that. I felt strangely alone. I picked up a rock or two so I'd feel better about myself.

I ended up running into Nick, Max, and Emily. Emily looked happy to see me this time. The rest of Emily's group – Sarah, Sarah, and Tessa – were also there. We all walked around a bit, and they sat and I took a couple of pictures of them. The six of them are sitting on a couple of benches in the middle of the plaza, looking tired but content. The snapshot of that moment in time is one of those great snapshots I have from this trip. It represents the contemplative and relaxed, but exhausting, mood of the day.

It was good to spend this time with the kids today. Most of my experiences in Europe have been with the adults, and a little bit with Emily, and we've certainly enjoyed our exchanges with the locals – and every bit of it has been fantastic. But I need to remember that there are others on this trip with us. After all, the others are the reason we're here.

I'm running out of money and am a little worried because no one in Rome seems to accept credit cards. I go across the street to get a gelato, but at the last minute I decide to skip it and come back. As I'm returning, the others decide to go over there for some refreshment, so I save their spots for them. When they return, Emily shares some of her gelato with me.

We wait a bit longer, and pretty soon the rest of the group joins us. We walk to our Rome dinner spot. It's called Testa del Roma or something like that. So far here, cuisine-wise, everything has been pasta, pizza and spam. The pasta tonight is good, but it's more of the same. (One Italian restaurant where we ate served a main dish of pizza, a pizza salad, and chocolate pizza for dessert.)

After dinner we board the coach and head back to the Villa Maria, our very nice motel. Kathie and I have a small balcony – nice, but not as large as some of the others and not as special as the one in Einsiedeln, or as exclusive. It's curious how we've been on the exact-same adventure this whole time, and yet we have felt (or *I* have felt) both incredibly privileged, and strangely inadequate. The accommodations have been mostly comfortable, but somewhat inconsistent. (We're at the mercy of our hosts.) This isn't a complaint; it's merely an observation. I want to remember everything.

Once again I met with Kathie, Dorinda and the others for a nightcap. Emily wanted a frappe, so I agreed to buy each of us one. After all, she shared her gelato with me earlier in the day! Then she went back up to her room and I stayed with the adults. It was a long day and everyone was tired, so we didn't stay downstairs for long.

6/29 -- Rome → Pompei, Italy

Today's drive was from Rome to Pompei (formerly Pompeii). We went there to see the ruins that remained following the eruption of Mt. Vesuvius in 79 A.D. We had the best guide yet on this trip. She was informative, funny and clear; she answered our questions and waited patiently for us when necessary. Very personable, too.

Another brief history lesson: Pompei is an archeological marvel. Gordy always told me how fascinating it was (he traveled here during his overseas Navy days), and he was absolutely right. The volcanic ash actually preserved the city as it was just before Vesuvius erupted. We saw mansions and small homes, all together. We walked through the "red light" district and got to see a brothel that had only been excavated for touring three years ago. I'd never seen a brothel before, and didn't know they were so plain. The beds were made of stone. Ow. I saw a couple of what were probably remains in an earlier tableau, but they, too, were embedded in stone.

We were all standing in an open area and the members of our group seemed to be peering off into the distance at I don't know what. I looked toward them (they were facing my way), and behind them I saw the mountain, which appeared to be a distant backdrop. It was the mountain that caused all the destruction and misery, but it looked so little and innocent that it was rather hard to believe. No one else looked at it or seemed to notice it until I asked the guide if that, indeed, was Mt. Vesuvius. "Yes," she answered, and her eyes laughed.

We checked into the Hotel Albatross outside of Sorrento. We had eaten lunch – pizza, salad, beverage, and gelato – at a "way station" in Pompei. Our nice guide, Pauline, doesn't trust other places to eat in Pompei and can't vouch for them. (We're outside of Naples now.) She said they agreed to accept credit from a limited number of people. However, as it was my hope to put my table on a credit card – giving me an extra 50€ -- they said (after lunch) no, we don't take credit.

I was no longer just worried about money at this point. I was angry. I wouldn't have eaten at all if I'd known, because there went another 10€. I'm down to 40€ - 50€ for the rest of the trip, and Emily's asking if she can borrow some of my money.

It's no one's fault but my own, really, but there's been a good deal of misinformation and miscommunication on this trip.

I didn't feel like writing about it at the time, but now I will. The other day, Angela and Daniel had a huge blowout. Pauline was there, too. I don't know what it was about, but I suspect it had something to do with different agendas for the two different busses.

The overseer of our bus felt that our riders were getting the short end of the deal. At the same time, she was surprisingly harsh with the students the other day. She would not allow them to go to a discotheque in Einsiedeln (outside Lucerne), even with adult supervision. It seemed arbitrary and unfair to me, because it had been preannounced as a student activity and they had wanted to go. They'd already been told that under no circumstances were they allowed to drink alcohol (the drinking age is 16 in these parts), and she was concerned that if given the chance, they would do it anyway. So, she put the kibosh on the discotheque.

As far as the money goes, well, let's just say that it goes awfully fast. I spent 20€ for Emily and me for the tour of Rome at night; 5-6€ for lunch in Assisi; 5€ for stamps at Assisi; 3€ for the coins at Trevi Fountain (3 coins); probably 4-5€ for gelato at a couple places; 15€ for beer; 8€ for frappe; and more. I should have kept better track. I also gave Angela 20€ for a tip for Nino, our bus driver in Italy. I think I gave somebody one Euro for water in Rome. That was actually a deal.

But, I digress. We bussed it from Pompei to Sorrento, a gorgeous resort city on the West Coast of Italy near the boot's inside shin; a point just south of Napoli (Naples) and on the mainland a stone's throw from the exquisite Mediterranean island of Capri. It's a tiny, tiny island and very opulent. Sorrento may be the most magnificent view city I've ever seen – just breathtaking in its beauty and serenity.

Kathie and I took a pleasant walk to the bank where I gathered more stones for Thomas (they had slipped into my shoe); and then to the grocery store where we bought a few food supplies and munchies. Kathie is the best company. Like all of these wonderful women, she's kind, gregarious, generous, warm, and funny. It's a real gift to be in the company of these people. I can't say enough good things about any of them.

Our hotel, the Hotel Albatross, was lovely. The flooring was of a pristine blue, yellow, and white mosaic tile in a cheerful design. The room, although small, was clean and elegant. It felt good to be here.

After check-in and a bit of settling-in, I went swimming in the Albatross' lovely swimming pool. The students had already gone swimming, so I had a chance to swim laps with Kathie, Sue and Jeff. After the swim, I took in a luxurious warm shower before dinner.

When I arrived in the lunchroom for the evening's supper, I saw that Emily was seated at another nice table. She looked contented and refreshed, which was exactly how I felt. Tonight's meal was delicious: a spicy rice dish, quite generous portions; green salad; grilled chicken; delicious French or sourdough bread with olive oil; fresh fruit (orange) for dessert; and – icing on the cake – red wine, *gracie* (compliments of) Kathie and Dorinda. I enjoyed the meal immensely and had a good time.

I decided to skip the night bus tour through Sorrento (where Pauline was going to reunite with her boyfriend of seventeen years) for two reasons: one, money (12€ that I could not afford to spend); and two, exhaustion bordering on fatigue. It was a pleasant exhaustion at that. I wasn't complaining.

Our leader told us we needed to tip Nino, our driver, because tomorrow (6/30) is his last day with us. Ten days at 1€ a day/person. That's 20€ for Em and me, and it must be paid in Euros, not credit. Of course. So, I paid it. I'm not usually grumpy about such things, but after all it was this same leader who had assured us before the trip that American credit was accepted all over Europe, no problem. Nothing against our driver Nino, whose company I appreciated, but at that particular moment I wasn't feeling the "love."

I was discussing my low cash situation with Dorinda, feeling a little better but still slightly worried. She said she was thinking of skipping the Sorrento night ride. She had already paid for it, so it wasn't the money. She was concerned about the rain and the steep hills, which seemed treacherous. I was happy but comfortably tired and felt just fine to be skipping it. Emily knew, and seemed disappointed that I wasn't going. She had paid to go herself, using what little funds she had left. I'd also told some of the others that I wasn't going on the night tour through Tuscany, and everyone was kind and sympathetic about it.

We had all finished eating and were enjoying time together before the night's excursion, and it was just a great time. Moods were light and cheerful. Dorinda said, "see you soon," and left.

I walked out to the hotel lobby to ask a question at the front desk, and saw Dorinda talking to Daniel. A moment later, Daniel came up to me and said my ride through Tuscany was taken care of for tonight. I said, "How?" and he said, "Don't ask." So I didn't. I just held my breath for a minute or two, unbelieving.

I went up and told Kathie I was going, and what happened, and she was funny – she said "bummer" because she knew I'd been looking forward to relaxing a little, doing some laundry, possibly catching a bit of Italian television or reading, and enjoying a much-needed, solid night's sleep. But I told Kathie that now that I had a free pass to go, I was excited to go! I felt special. Throughout this trip, I've been reading *What Happy People Know*. Gratitude is the key to happiness, and gratitude is exactly what I feel.

The Happiness book has been a consistent reminder of my debt of gratitude and appreciation, as well as love, for these wonderful people and this huge opportunity. I like to make jokes about it and I've gotten grumpy at times, increasingly finding myself in situations that are outside of my comfort zone, but overall I feel extremely blessed.

Sorrento has been the absolute highlight of this entire trip, which is saying a lot, since I nearly didn't go. The drive was amazing, of course. Emily and I got some pictures plus Tessa sweetly asked me to take pictures of her and her friends, and I was glad to do so.

Emily was surprised to see me when we all got off the bus. (We were on different buses.) I was on a crowded bus but it was a good one. I sat in the back row next to Carol, who is just a sweetheart. Dorinda sat in the row in front of us; students Max, Stephanie, and Thomas were sitting toward the back as well. Another student, Louis, was there and said hi; glad I made it. He had even offered to pay for me earlier, but I had politely declined the offer.

Dorinda said she was glad I made it, too. I felt touched to be there the entire time; it was like a dream. I know now that I have a guardian angel looking out for me, and her name is Dorinda.

Kathie is an angel, too: she took out an extra 50€ at the ATM and loaned it to me for the rest of the trip!

(The bus is jittery and I'm probably misspelling names and things. I only mention it because I can't believe any of this is legible.)

And Daniel, finally, was an angel on this trip. We did a little shopping and I bought three small, adorable bottles of olive oil (chili, garlic and rosemary) from an adorable elderly, intelligent and frustrated shopkeeper who scolded me for not paying attention when he was trying to tell me the differences between olive oils. I listened to him (despite what he thought), thanked him and bought three bottles with my credit card -- 9€ total.

We also enjoyed free samples of Limoncello, a lemon liqueur. Not to my liking, but interesting – especially since I do love lemon. Lemonade without the alcohol would have been just fine with me. But the two shopkeepers who waited on us were characters, and I appreciated them. *Gracie* and *arrivederci*!

As we left the lovely, quaint cobblestone of shops, and rounded the corner toward a more commercial block, we spotted Daniel. He directed us to an exclusive lounge that, according to Daniel, has a sort-of "members only" policy: it only caters to elite locals, and to exclusive guests and their parties. It's similar to the atmosphere at Salty's Restaurant, only it's so much better because it's hidden, surprisingly unpretentious, boasts a gorgeous drop-dead view overlooking the Bay of Salerno, and to top it off, its prices are amazingly reasonable.

Other amenities include excellent and pleasant service, free small appetizers, and plenty of seating. I believe it's called Foreigners Lounge -- I was having such a good time that I forgot to confirm this. Foreigners Lounge would be an apropos name for it, because the staff was easygoing and friendly toward us foreigners; we felt relaxed and unhurried. The establishment has the feel of a very cultured country club, but it is also low-key. I was home there. Of course, the agreeable company had a lot to do with that.

We spent a good hour-plus basking in the view, surroundings, kind service, and delicious cold beers. Terry, Sue, Dorinda, Kathie, Denise, and I were there. We'd lost Mel from the corner shop (olive oil shop) to the lounge – she was happy at the corner shop, but went her own way after that. Because of Kathie's earlier largesse of the 50€ loan, I easily paid the 5€ as my portion of the bar bill. I don't even remember a night when I've felt this good, and that's saying a lot.

Earlier today, I sent postcards to my friends Paula and Maydene. Both cards were of Assisi. I told Paula that young Max said to say hi.

We returned late (around midnight) and for once, went straight up to our respective rooms. No more beers tonight. We were all contentedly exhausted, thank God.

6/30 -- Sorrento, Italy → Ferry boat to Athens, Greece

We're traveling by bus from Sorrento, Italy to the ferry that will take us to Athens. It's been described as "basic" but clean and moderately accommodating. Don't expect the Queen Mary, we're told. We're driving alongside the Adriatic Sea.

The bank wouldn't accept my credit card for cash exchange this morning, but Daniel said I could put the (later) trip to Turkey on my credit card, add a couple of people onto the card, and collect cash from them. This will work. Pauline – did I mention this already? – was happy to see her boyfriend in Sorrento. Her birthday is July 2nd.

The bus ride is okay so far. We stopped for lunch and I bought Emily's. At a rest stop, I took a picture of our driver, Nino, and thanked him for all he had done for us.

We boarded the ferry around 6:00 for a 7:00 p.m. departure. It was much lovelier than I expected it to be – new, clean, fairly roomy and with more amenities than I expected – almost like a small cruise ship. It was from the Endeavor Steamship Company. They had a cafeteria, several bars, disco, cinema, casino and shops onboard. The sunset was stunning; I snapped a picture of it. The adults enjoyed wine and good conversation, and I took a very pleasant stroll around the deck of the ferry boat a couple of times.

Dinner was some sort of stroganoff, a salad, and Diet Coke. Pretty good. I went to bed around 11:00-midnight and slept until 5:30 a.m.

7/1 -- Ferry boat to Athens → Athens, Greece

Our continental breakfast on the ferry boat consisted of coffee, juice, bread and butter. We disembarked and boarded a new bus for Kalambaka, Greece. We stopped for lunch, where I had a delicious Greek salad. I sat with Dorinda, Terry and Sue, and they allowed me to put the bill on a card while they each paid me in Euros. That helped.

We also toured a couple of monasteries. Both poor and opulent. I wasn't sure how I felt about that or what statement it made. The atmosphere is rich, but those who frequent it are anything but. The monks can and frequently do (but are not required to) make a lifetime commitment to the monastery. Their lives consist of a strict schedule: eight hours of work, 8 hours of prayer, and 8 hours of sleep a day. I wonder when they eat. I wonder when they play. But they are allowed to vacation and see their families.

Today we are staying at a lovely hotel called the Hotel Famissi. Kathie and I checked in and then took our laundry to the one-day cleaner/laundromat (8€ a bag). Then we went exploring, and stopped for beers with Sue, Terry and Jeff. Dorinda joined us later. Fun!

Emily is being elusive again. I don't know why. I bought another deck of playing cards for Thomas – Athens cards, 2€. No one seems to take credit here – not the bars, not the cleaners, not the shopkeepers, and probably not the bakeries. Dang. It's a good thing I have a little more cash now!

Dinner consisted of salad, a very tender side of chicken (delicious), rice and veggies (peas and carrots), and juicy watermelon for dessert. It was all very good, and the dining room is roomy and elegant here at the hotel. Emily sat with her entire group at dinner tonight, plus Nick, Max and Kirk. I was glad to see her sitting with that group, because sometimes she prefers to go it alone. At times it appeared to me that she was distancing herself from her group, so I asked Kathie and Sue (who both went through this teenage phase with their older kids) what they would do. They suggested it was just a teenage thing and to just ignore it for now, i.e. don't draw attention to it because it will probably only make things worse. So, that is what I am doing for the time being.

After the yummy dinner, Kathie and I ventured out for more shopping, where I bought two new pairs of earrings as gifts for people back home. Then, we joined up with Dorinda for beers.

7/2 -- Athens/Delphi, Greece

It's Pauline's birthday today. We coached from Kalambaka and will be in Athens tonight. We'll be staying at the Hotel Oscar. We will also take in a side trip to Delphi.

We stopped for lunch, where I was overcharged 3€. I was charged for a 6€ lunch and a 3€ drink, but I didn't get a drink. Since it was a pre-charge, I paid the 9€ before realizing that the meal I bought was only 6€. But I didn't feel too bad about it, because I also put Denise's and Kathie's lunches on my credit card (yes!!- they actually accepted credit).

We got back on the bus and made our way to Delphi, where we had a really interesting but slippery (walking stones) tour. I nearly fell twice. And my knee is killing me. I picked up one of the evil stones and added it to my rock collection.

The hotel in Athens, Hotel Oscar, is located in what can only be described as a slum. The hotel itself looks like faded opulence – perhaps, like the Milford Plaza in Manhattan, it has seen better days and it does boast a rooftop swimming pool, but it is definitely frayed around the edges – slightly dingy despite (or maybe because of) the overly elaborate lobby chandeliers. It reminds me of the Overlook Hotel in *The Shining.* I suspect it harbors secrets I'd rather not have revealed. We only stayed there one night.

Huge drama tonight. It was an argument between two of our leaders about the bus driver's tip. Both of these leaders are very unhappy right now. One thought the tip was too high; the other thought it wasn't enough. Our leader embroiled all of the adults in the drama, which I thought was inappropriate. If it were such a concern, they should have included a gratuity in everyone's total travel bill and been done with it. You can't expect to ask 16-year-old students to come up with a two-week tip the night before it's due, especially when money is so tight at this point. (There are only four adult parents accompanying their kids on this trip. I'm one of them.)

The day ended with all of us singing "Happy Birthday" to Pauline, so at least it ended on a positive note!

7/3 -- Athens → Greek Islands/Mykonos, Potnos, Santorini; with side trips to Knossos (Crete) in Greece and to Ephesus, Turkey

We departed Athens for our Greek cruise on the M/V Easy Cruise Line. Not a minute too soon, either, on account of last night's drama and our weird, borderline-creepy hotel stay. Our ship is wonderful, and it's called the *Valletta.*

Our first stop is Mykonos. I walked along the beach there with Dorinda, Kathie, and possibly Denise, while the others took the bus. I bought a large blue bag that says *Mykonos* across the front. We had beers at a wonderful outdoor restaurant. I could get so used to this lifestyle, if only I could afford it -- and if I had the rest of my family here.

Around this point in the trip I started to lose track of the time, but while in Greece we made a morning excursion to Ephesus, Turkey. We saw a Turkish rug tour, and we got to see the last home of Jesus' mother Mary before she died. People who I've read about my entire life actually lived here in ancient times, before the birth of Christ (obviously). Knowing that they lived at all was validating.

7/4 -- Knossos (Crete) and the island of Potnos, Greece

Emily joined me for an excursion to Knossos. Only seven people attended this particular trip – Kathie and Kirk (yay), Mel, Carol, and John. We saw cave pictures of the Minotaur, a mythical monster that resembles a bull. We toured a once-civilized area in Knossos that boasted the first indoor plumbing in ancient times. Although it's now in ruins, you can still see remnants of the indoor plumbing. It was quite the achievement. I can't believe the others missed this!

I have a burn from swimming, hot-tubbing and lying in the sun on the deck of the ship (that was yesterday). It's especially angry around my ankles. Several people have remarked about how bad it looks. And it hurts.

We stopped at Potnos, another small, lovely island resort. We went swimming on the beach. Emily looked adorable in her cute beach outfit. I swam and back-floated in the water; lovely. Gordy had warned me against swimming in the Aegean Sea, but here I am and you know what they say when in Rome...or Potnos. Besides, there are no predictions of underwater earthquakes today. On the way back to our ship, I stopped for a quick lunch and bought a few souvenirs for the folks back home. Then we set sail for Santorini, which will be our final island stop in Greece.

We enjoyed a delicious buffet dinner on the ship. Shipboard meals are the best, and since we prepaid for the Greek cruise, I don't have to pull out cash or a credit card! Whew.

Later I had drinks on the pool deck with Denise, Kathie, Dorinda, Terry, and Sue. It was another great day and evening. Also, this was "Greek night" with dancing! Kind of a free-for-all. Everyone got on the dance floor and had fun; it wasn't a "couples" sort of thing, at least in our group.

7/5 – Santorini, Greece

I didn't disembark in Santorini. I figured that if you've seen one Greek island, you've seen them all. Okay, that's a lie. The reason I didn't go was that this was an add-on trip, and I had run out of money. So, instead of taking the day's excursion, I took photos from the port bow of the cruise boat/water taxi to the *coast* of Santorini. I watched the cable cars as they carried the passengers up a windy hill, and then I went inside and took a nice nap.

Later, or maybe earlier (like I said, I'm starting to lose track of time) I took a refreshing dip in the ship's comfortable pool. I had it all to myself! The group returned around 8:00 p.m. for dinner. Best yet. I stayed up until about 11:30, packed and turned in for our final night on the cruise ship. I loved this cruise, even with the occasional mini-dramas happening. And although Emily and I have had our ups and downs throughout this European vacation (understandable, considering that most of the other students were traveling without their parents), we're getting along well now. I'm feeling happy.

Emily remarked at dinner that I really should have gone to Santorini, because it was by far the best of the Greek islands. It has those rows of lovely white homes and temple structures with the blue-domed rooftops that you see in all the calendars and brochures of the Greek islands. Santorini was represented in the movie *The Sisterhood of the Traveling Pants*, as well as a few others. I'm feeling a little bummed for having missed it now. Oh well, maybe next time….

7/6 -- Greek Islands → Athens

We disembarked in Athens and took a tour of the Parthenon, Acropolis, and Parliament. Athens appears to be the most ancient of the ancient cities in Europe, although technically, I don't know if it is. It might be Rome. (I'll have to brush up on my ancient history.) We saw the five rings of the Olympics, which originated in Athens. And then – gag me! -- we stopped for coffee at Mickey D's (a first and last on this trip). I'm kind of ashamed about it, because I had made a point of *not* going to a McDonald's the entire time we were in Europe. Oh, well -- it's our last day and it's only a cup of coffee.

Well, at least I have rocks from all the places in Athens (and elsewhere) that we visited. Thomas will be pleased! The only downside is that the rocks have weighted down my luggage quite a bit, but it would be a shame to part with them now.

We stopped at the Hard Rock Café on our way back to our bus, but I didn't buy anything there. When we got to the bus, I discovered to my dismay that Emily's group hadn't shown up yet. I was worried, because everyone else was there and waiting. Until now, Emily's small group has always arrived promptly for field excursions and bus trips. In addition -- despite my personal perception of her somewhat sullen demeanor on several occasions -- her group has managed to avoid any needless drama this whole time.

During the Greek cruise, several of the instructors and chaperones remarked that Emily's was the most reliable and well-behaved group on this tour. While this was music to my ears at the time, it was suddenly cause for concern.

Kirk agreed to look for the girls at an outdoor fountain a few blocks from the Hard Rock Café. It was the last place where they were spotted. He ran there, but they showed up while he was gone and he was the last one back. He did the right thing, and I appreciate him so much for it. And he still made it back in time, with two minutes to spare!

After the bus ride, we checked into the Hotel London near the Athens beach (Aegean Sea). Kathie, Dorinda, Sam, Angela, Jeff, Joclyn, Katy and I walked to the beach and admired the beautiful warm water. We had lunch at a funky outdoor beach café (Kathie, Denise, Dorinda, and me). We had beers and shared cheese pies, burgers, fries, fried zucchini, and calamari. Then, we had a beach swim. Don't ask me how we managed it. The rocks on the beach hurt my feet and I was chicken, but once I was in the water it was great swimming. After swimming, I grabbed another rock for Thomas (can't help myself – I'm obsessed) and we all went back for dinner. Burp...I ate light.

7/7 -- Athens, Greece → Newark, NJ, USA → Seattle, WA, USA

We had a scrumptious breakfast this morning – our last one overseas. Now, we're on our final bus ride to the airport. Our plane will arrive in Seattle at 9:31 a.m. on 7/7. That's not a typo. We'll arrive in Seattle on the morning of the same day we departed Athens. It's an overnight flight with a big time difference, and we'll gain time on the return flight.

Emily and I are both feeling a little subdued about the vacation's conclusion, but we're also feeling excited about returning home.

7/7 – Seattle, WA, USA

Gordy and Thomas picked us up at the airport. When we arrived home, it was so good to see the house and to greet the kitties, who were ecstatic for Emily's return! Gordy prepared for us a delicious dinner (not pasta – thank you, God). It consisted of steak, mashed potatoes, a salad with all the fixings, and sourdough rolls with butter.

For dessert, Gordy presented a chocolate cake that he had designed and custom-ordered. It was very cleverly frosted with flags of all the countries we visited: England, France, Switzerland, Italy, Vatican City, Greece, and Turkey. Delicious! And fun. Emily and I talked about the trip a little…but when Thomas told Emily about the fishing trip he took with Dad while we were in Europe, Emily became jealous. Thomas said he would agree to trade with her next time. Big of him!

Staring at that remarkable cake before dissecting it, I was happily reminded of all the fascinating places we visited. I recalled so many first-time adventures and the pure, giddy fun of the last twenty days.

I thought back on the fear that I might run out of money, and how lucky and relieved I felt that that didn't happen. I remembered the torrential rainstorm in Florence, where I nearly fell on my face a couple times (in Delphi, too). I worried about my poor knees, which felt like they had rocks in them. Good times.

I was grateful for the friends I made overseas – not just those from Europe, but those I spent time with who live right here in Seattle, and who I will gladly see again. And I was particularly delighted to have shared this enormous adventure with Emily. I think we both learned a great deal from it, and the experience has brought us closer together. It has done wonders for her.

Although I'd love to go back someday, there's nothing like the simple pleasure of being home. I can't *wait* to sleep in my own bed. I even look forward to unpacking all the stones I collected for Thomas during my travels. Each stone is labeled by location and date, and each is individually wrapped inside a napkin or paper towel. When I unfold them, it will be fun to relive each place we visited.

There will be time enough for that tomorrow. Right now, *just to be here* is Heaven on earth. To be here is all I want.

www.ingramcontent.com/pod-product-compliance
Lightning Source LLC
Chambersburg PA
CBHW030938180526
45163CB00002B/622